WHY THIS BOOK CAN HELP YOU GET THIN AND STAY THAT WAY FOREVER

How often have you gone on a diet, with or without the aid of the latest best-seller on the subject, only to gain back, all too soon, every pound you painfully took off? The fact is that until you learn what obesity *really* is, and until you learn why you *really* overeat, you are a blind man searching in a dark room for a black cat that isn't there.

And along with everything else, you must learn the strangest and most significant lesson of all. You must learn to accept the fact that, incredible as it sounds, you are unconsciously *afraid* of becoming thin. You must learn why this is so—and what you can do about it. That is what this book is all about.

FOREVER THIN

Theodore Isaac Rubin, M.D.

A BERKLEY MEDALLION BOOK
PUBLISHED BY
BERKLEY PUBLISHING CORPORATION

To fat men and women everywhere:
How well I understand the struggle.

Library of Congress
Catalog Card Number: 76-113939
SBN 425-02763-5

BERKLEY MEDALLION BOOKS are published by
Berkley Publishing Corporation
200 Madison Avenue
New York, N.Y. 10016

BERKLEY MEDALLION BOOKS ® TN 757,375

Printed in the United States of America

Berkley Medallion Edition, FEBRUARY, 1975

FOURTH PRINTING

"And homeless near a thousand homes I stood,
And near a thousand tables pined and wanted food."

from "Guilt and Sorrow"
by William Wordsworth

CONTENTS

PART III. OVERCOMING OBESITY AND THE FEAR OF BECOMING AND STAYING THIN

PART IV. WHAT YOU SHOULD KNOW ABOUT YOURSELF

PREFACE

This book can help you lose weight and stay at your ideal level more effectively than any ten diet books put together. I say that because, unless you learn the psychological principles set forth in this volume, those diet books will be of no real value to you.

You know this yourself. How often have you gone on a diet, with or without the aid of the latest best seller on the subject, only to gain back, all too soon, every pound you painfully took off? The fact is that until you learn what obesity *really* is, and until you learn *why* you really overeat, you are like a blind man searching in a dark room for a black cat that isn't there.

And along with everything else, you must learn the strangest and most significant lesson of all. You must learn to accept the fact that, incredible as it sounds, you are unconsciously *afraid* of becoming thin. You must learn why this is so—and what you can do about it.

Going on a diet *before* you learn the basic precepts taught in *Forever Thin* is pretty sure to prove a waste of time. But once you learn them, then any sound diet will do wonders for you, and you will indeed be able to become a living, walking personification of the title by becoming thin—whether you want to lose ten pounds or fifty—and *staying* that way the rest of your life.

This is not the first time I have dealt with the psychology of fatness, but this book goes much further than its predecessor. In *The Thin Book by a Formerly Fat Psychiatrist* (Trident Press), I detailed a practical way of emotionally campaigning against fatness. That book tells how to get on a diet and how to stay on one and deals with the emotional factors involved.

This book, *Forever Thin,* deals with the underlying emotional nature and causes of fatness. Of course there will be some over-lapping, but this book is primarily concerned with the psychodynamics of obesity. Understanding this condition is crucial to success. By success, I mean losing weight—but much more than that, I also mean sustaining the weight loss and staying thin.

The vast majority of fat people lose weight again and again and again because they gain it back again and again and again. This is so because they have little or no understanding of the emotional or psychological aspects of the condition or its control. The tons of material written on the subject almost in-variably deal with physiological and physical aspects of fatness and dieting. This goes on despite the fact that we are dealing with a condition that almost invariably has its basis in psychological roots.

Ignorance of emotional factors in a condition rooted in emotional disturbance can only lead to repeated failure. Successful and healthy control of any chronic condition—rheumatic fever, diabetes, or obesity—is immensely aided by insight into that condition. I try to provide some of that insight in this book.

After defining a few important terms, the book is divided into three parts designed to help you recognize, understand, and overcome the problem of obesity, with a final section of questions. Much of this material is gleaned from experience with patients I have treated, as well as from my own personal confrontation with obesity. After being fat for many years, I am happy to report, at this writing, that I have now been thin for many years. I wish you similar success.

Theodore Isaac Rubin, M.D.

PART I

RECOGNIZING OBESITY

FATNESS: OBESITY AND OVERWEIGHT

For the moment, please forget dictionary definitions. For our purposes, let us divide fatness into two categories: 1) Obesity and 2) Overweight.

Obesity *is the term we will use to designate the neurotic psychological condition that causes overeating, which in turn results in the physical condition,* overweight. *This, in effect, means that a person can have an obese state of mind even though he is no longer overweight. Again, purely for our purposes, anyone suffers from fatness whose psychological state is one of obesity, which leads to overeating and overweight. Please remember that from now on, when I speak of obesity I am speaking about the psychology of the fat individual.*

Naturally, the psychology of all people is highly individual. Each person has his own particular characteristics and, of course, problems vary in degree as well as in kind. But I think that you will find that most fat people have a great deal more in common than their overweight. Their obesity or emotional outlooks, their fatness psychologies, are very similar and in many ways are often identical. To lose weight and especially to sustain the weight loss, it is imperative to understand this obesity, this fatness psychology.

For our purpose I want to use and differentiate two more terms. Obesity thins will refer to people who have an obesity psychology but who are currently at their normal weight. Thin thins or True thins (I use these terms interchangeably) are people who are normally thin and who do not have an obesity psychology.

In our terms, temporary weight gain does not imply obesity. True thins can sometimes gain "too much weight" for a short period of time. By our definition, obesity is the psychological condition that leads to overeating and overweight (ten percent or more than the normally accepted weight for your size) for a period of at least ten years.

THE OBESITY PROFILE

We know too well about the physical profile of the fat person. We now also know that the obese individual has at one or another times in his life been ten or more pounds overweight for at least ten years. What else differentiates obese people from true thins? In the following six chapters I will briefly describe the unmistakable signs of the condition. It is important to recognize these signs and to understand as much about them as possible. This is so because, first it is disastrous to labor under the delusion that you are not obese when in fact you are. Secondly, it is important to familiarize yourself with these characteristics so as to better understand how they fit into and feed the whole obese way of life.

PREOCCUPATION WITH FOOD AND WEIGHT

This involvement with food, diets, and weight can be subtle or blatant, mild or severe, *but* it is always present in one or another forms when obesity is present. It can be part and parcel of one's thoughts, day-dreams, sleep dreams, conversations, or reading interests. Obese people, however ruthless they may seem in their attack on food, are in fact always conscious of themselves vis-à-vis food and eating. More often than not, they swing from concentration on dieting, food censorship, and weight loss or gain to anticipation of feasting to come and a devil-may-care attitude toward eating with limitless abandon. *But* a quarter of a day does not pass without considerable attention to food, either through thought, word, or deed or all three. This is not so with true thins. They simply cannot be bothered with the whole food thing. They may enjoy it, when they eat, but food occupies very little importance in the true-thin scheme of things.

Obese people, however thin they may be for however long, are always conscious of the quantities of food they are eating. Some are also aware of the fact that they can become fat again even after twenty years of extreme thinness. Obese people may seem as though they have no regard for quantity. They may overeat with what looks like abandon. But they are aware, and this consciousness of caloric quality and quantity is always present.

True thins eat without regard for quantity. They may or may not overeat, but they always eat spontaneously without consciousness or feelings about amounts or calories. For the most part they "know" when to stop—but more about this later. Suffice here to say that unlike true thins, obese people—however thin—cannot just forget about food and merely eat. They may appear to eat more or less freely, but they always have some awareness and feelings about food and eating that precludes the possibility of eating with spontaneous freedom.

Let me give you an example involving a patient of mine (an obese thin) and his friend (a true thin). I'll tell it in the first person from my patient's point of view:

"We had an appointment at 12:30 in his office to discuss some business. On the morning of the day of the appointment I thought about lunch several times. Would we eat in his office? Would we go out and eat? If so, when, where, and what. . . . Later on, I found out that he didn't think about it at all. I arrived at his office at 12:30 with mild misgivings. I was already hungry and felt that if lunch were delayed too long, I would become tired, irritable, and uncomfortably hungry. I had adequate experience to substantiate these feelings.

"We immediately sat down and discussed business, but I was only half there since I couldn't stop thinking about food and feeling sorry that I hadn't 'eaten a little something' on the way over. My friend later confirmed that he hadn't thought of food at all. As a matter of fact, he completely forgot about lunch.

"At 1:30 his secretary returned from her lunch and popped in to ask if she could send out for our lunch. My friend looked to me and I eagerly said, 'Sure, sure, by all means.' My friend ordered 'anything at all.' His secretary suggested a hamburger and coffee and he said, 'Fine.' She then looked to me. By this time I was feeling particularly sorry for myself in my acute hungry state. I therefore felt entitled to a special treat. After a good deal of deliberation and conflict I ordered a pastrami sandwich, a portion of potato salad, and a large Coca-Cola (nondiet), all of which were prohibited by my diet of that particular moment.

"Waiting for the food, my friend made several heroic efforts to continue with our talk. They were largely ineffectual since I was completely preoccupied with fantasies of pastrami. I should have ordered it on club bread. Did I or didn't I tell her to order it lean? When the food arrived, I ate it up, all of it, in five minutes. We then continued our discussion. My friend took an occasional small bite from his hamburger and eventually finished his coffee. Toward the end of the discussion he caught me eyeing his few potato chips and pickle (unordered, they arrived with the burger). He offered them to me and I ate them. I didn't dare eye his remaining burger, but did feel a sense of loss when he threw it into the wastebasket as our meeting ended and I left.

"On the elevator going down, I thought of heading for the nearest hamburger stand but suddenly had a heartburn, decided against it, and felt very noble. On the way home from work that evening I had mixed feelings about dinner. Should I go back on my diet immediately? Or as long as I already broke the diet at lunch, should I go on and eat whatever I liked this evening and make a new start in the morning? I felt my belly. I didn't want to gain it all back. But it was a hard decision to have to make."

In addition to food preoccupation, there is also the omnipresent weight factor, Again, obese people may seem not to care about their weight. Some few can even pass a scale with nary a glance in its direction. Well, don't believe it! This is conscious and contrived avoidance. True thins couldn't care less. Obese people always care, even though they may be helpless to do anything about it or pretend not to care. Of course, some are very frightened of scales and mirrors or even reflecting store windows, but they all care and are enormously conscious of scales, mirrors, and weight. Indeed, a great many feel compelled to weigh themselves a dozen times a day, and there are quite a few I've met who wake up to weigh themselves several times a night, too.

3

ENOUGH IS ENOUGH

True thins know when they've had enough food. They don't have to think about it, impose willpower, or do anything else. They just know. They eat for a while and then stop—spontaneously and automatically. Actually, nobody really knows why. I call this phenomenon the "enough is enough factor," or the *EEF*.

Some experts feel that this ability to know when one has had enough food is based on an inborn physiological mechanism that is working normally. It is felt that when the blood-sugar level, derived from adequate food intake into the digestive tract, has reached a normal critical level, this in turn stimulates a mechanism in the brain that lets the person know—by making him feel it—that he has had enough. Others say that fullness in the stomach produces this effect and have demonstrated their theory by inflating balloons in subjects' stomachs, attempting to thus negate hunger.

But still others believe that knowing when enough is enough is largely a psychological function. They feel that this sense of having enough is learned from one's earliest years and then continues to operate as a conditioned reflex. People are taught to feel that they have had enough and to stop eating when adequate amounts have been ingested. This psychological theory has been substantiated by researchers who show that obese people have a history of poor training or food stuffing that often goes back to infancy.

I feel that there are undoubtedly elements of both physiological and psychological factors present. Perhaps normal neurological responses are damaged and irreparably blunted by years of overstuffing so that the victim forever loses the ability to spontaneously, effortlessly, and automatically feel that he is full. In any case, obese people do not know or feel that enough is enough as true thins do.

In interviewing many obese thins, I have yet to be satisfied that they have developed the real *enough is enough factor* as true thins know it. Compensatory steps *can* be taken to make up for this lack, however, and I shall talk more about this very important aspect later.

Let me tell you of a simple "test," which you yourself undoubtedly have taken part in many times. I call it the *Mashed Potato-Spaghetti-Rice Test:* We will assume that there are unwitting and untrained obese people (who have not learned to compensate for lack of the EEF) and true thins at the table.

A huge amount of food is placed on the table. It should meet three requirements: 1) Everybody likes it; 2) It is a food that is served in bulk rather than by the piece (mashed potatoes rather than individual baked potatoes—so that nobody can count and become self-conscious); 3) It should be served in a huge quantity so that it cannot possibly be finished nor can continued and large self-helpings produce embarrassment.

Now watch as the true thins eat and stop as relatively small amounts are ingested. The obese people, thin or fat (assuming they are not on a regimen and have not compensated for their EEF lack), will eat "too much." Some of them will eat huge portions. Others will go on eating and nibbling long after everyone else has stopped. Some will do both. In any case, it will usually be easy to distinguish those who have an EEF operating from those whose EEF is totally impaired or is simply lacking.

Lack of the EEF can result in from moderate to severe overeating. There are people who eat themselves into absolute stupors and even unto death. Much depends on what compensatory education exists, as well as the individual's psychology at a given time. I will discuss these factors later. Suffice now to say that people who are unconsciously self-destructive, who lack the EEF, who do not have insight as regards this factor, and who do not train and compensate accordingly are always in a highly precarious position.

4

MOUTH HUNGER

Being hungry and feeling hungry must be differentiated from "mouth hunger," which is always present in obese people. Tissues need food to sustain life, and the extraordinarily complicated and wonderful mechanism that produces hunger, which tells us to seek food, largely makes life possible. *Mouth hunger* is not related to the physiological need for food necessary to sustain life. Indeed, mouth hunger is often present when the physiological need for food (that is, tissue hunger) is entirely absent.

What I choose to call mouth hunger or MH relates to a great concentration of feelings, appetites, and sensations centered on or about the mouth. I include the lips, tongue, and oral cavity. Obese people are mouth-hungry people. They always have a much higher MH index than true thins or the rest of the population. They are capable of much mouth sensitivity, which may range from relatively subtle feelings to those that are quite sensational and even exquisitely sensual.

Feelings on, around, and in the mouth can

be highly varied in nature and can make one
desirous of making the mouth move, of feeling friction against the tongue, the insides of
the mouth, against the lips, and so on.
Mouth-hungry people satisfy many of these
yearnings by much random mouth moving,
talking, and eating. You undoubtedly know
people who suck in their cheeks, constantly
explore their mouths and lips with their
tongues, rub their lips together, smack their
lips, wet their lips, clean their teeth with lips
and tongue, and some who talk constantly
and some who overeat.

But mouth-hungry people also displace
many other feelings, appetites, and
frustrations to their mouths. Since food
offers the possibility of much immediate
mouth activity and mouth function and
fullness, it is easy to see how all kinds of
emotional needs are displaced to food and to
the mouth. We will explore this idea more
fully in Part II, the section on understanding.

A high MH index is always present in
obese people. Let me describe several
characteristics that are always present in
such people:

Mouth-hungry people talk a lot, and very
often they talk about food. They also salivate
easily and profusely and are highly im-
aginative and suggestible. They therefore
differ from true thins in that talking does
not dry the mouth but rather stimulates it to
seek more action. Talk of food brings on
food fantasies, much salivation, and food
craving. Since they are highly suggestible,

talk of food or talk of hunger will bring on immediate empathetic yearnings for food. Obese people who are highly mouth hungry will seldom turn down an unplanned invitation to eat. If food is anywhere about or if the aroma is anywhere in the air (and their olfactory ability is usually excellent as regards food), they will initiate the invitation themselves. If anyone is looking for a partner to join him for a sandwich or an impromptu dinner feast, he can almost always count on the mouth-hungry obese person to join him (unless he is in the middle of a successfully working regimen).

Mouth-hungry people are also impulse eaters. They need no plan or, for that matter, any purpose. This means that they do not have to be hungry in order to eat. The mere presence or possibility or even talk or fantasy of food is enough to bring on sufficient appetite to eat.

People with a high MH index (all obese people) will also eat nearly anything that is edible. Actually if nothing else is around, they will often eat things that they don't at all like. They may be very fine in their tastes and extremely discriminate in their ability to discern good cooking. Some of them are gourmet cooks as well as eaters, but this does not stop them from eating indiscriminately. I have known obese people who are gourmets and yet who eat—with disgust—food that they despise and know will make them sick. This is always followed by much self-recrimination.

This impulsive, indiscriminate eating

often leads to great bloating, indigestion, heartburn, and even physical conditions of a much more serious nature, as well as to immediate promises of "not to eat that garbage again," "not to overeat again," etc.—all of which are immediately broken. Obviously, this kind of eating is not only *imp*ulsive in nature, but *comp*ulsive as well. These people simply can't say no to themselves or anyone else. They are driven by great mouth hunger and also by unconscious needs displaced to the mouth, about which I will say more a little later on.

Before I close this chapter, I want to mention one more characteristic of mouth-hungry people that is also part and parcel of food preoccupation. Since food is the fuel that both satisfies and stimulates mouth hunger, obese people tend to measure events, time, parties, and so on, in terms of food. Here are some typical statements: "Yes, I remember when that happened—it was the day we ate all of those hamburgers." "That was a great wedding—wonderful roast beef." "I love to go to the ballgames and races and eat those terrific boiled frankfurters." "New York is a great city— any kind of food you want day or night." "Gee, some of the wonderful times we used to have when we were kids. I remember those great feasts my mother made—tons of mashed potatoes, yams, chocolate graham-cracker pudding—great times." No matter what their memories for ordinary things are like, obese people nearly always have superb "food memories." They will, in a pinch, invariably remember a rich birthday cake stored in a freezer six months earlier or the exact spot where excellent egg rolls may be bought—however deficient their sense of direction happens to be in nonfood matters.

5

FOOD ADDICTION

Food addiction is another very important characteristic of the obesity profile. It is virtually impossible for the obese person to eat just a little food—to take just a taste of something—when still more is available. The food addict must see it through; that is, he must eat up just about all that is available to him. If he is stopped precipitously for whatever reason, he will have to exert considerable control to not have a temper tantrum. If the food is removed precipitously, it will be hard for him to think of anything else so long as he knows that it still exists in edible form anywhere in the available vicinity.

The addict finds it almost impossible to go on discretionary diets in which he is permitted the responsibility of choice or direction. He can operate only where boundaries are fixed in an all-or-nothing way designating specific foods and amounts.

Unlike true thins, food, rather than producing satiation, stimulates the addict's appetite
for more food.

This is especially true of particular foods,
depending on the particular addict involved. There are many addicts who are
particularly vulnerable to sweet foods, and
especially to chocolate. Many of these people
have responses quite similar to that of
certain alcoholics. They can abstain from
chocolate sometimes even when it is present
in the same room with them. But should the
addict taste—merely taste—the addicting
food, an overwhelming and insurmountable
"need" for the food in question will be ini-
tiated. His mouth hunger at this time will
become unbearable, and he will feel that it
can be relieved only by huge quantities of the
"offending" substance. I have known
chocolate addicts who have eaten five
pounds of chocolate at a single sitting. I had
one patient in treatment, an ice cream
addict, who once went through two gallons
of ice cream without a stop.

Interestingly, following this kind of bout,
these people often experience a type of
nausea, bloatedness, stupor, and euphoria
not unlike the drunkenness experienced by
alcoholics. I had one patient who insisted
that she "got drunk on food." This is no
surprise when we realize that both food and
alcohol addicts have common difficulties in
relating to themselves and to other people.

One of the greatest difficulties they share
is an inability to handle anger. Both groups
are invariably very angry people with

remarkably little awareness of their anger or the ways they pervert it. One group uses food, the other alcohol, both trying to anesthetize feelings, especially angry feelings.

Food addiction is in its way more difficult to cope with than alcohol, drugs, or tobacco. This is so because we can live very well without any alcohol, drugs, or tobacco at all, but we must have food to survive. Complete abstinence is much easier than partial withdrawal. I know many obese people who find it much easier to go on a complete starvation diet than on any kind of low calorie diet. This is of course due to the fact that any contact with the addictive substance immediately brings on a desire for more and more and still more.

This desire for more is further enhanced by the black-and-white way in which most obese people operate. Their very common feeling is expressed by the statement, "Well, I ate a little something and the next thing I thought was, I may as well go all the way and eat all I want. . . . I'll go on a complete diet tomorrow." Of course, any break in the diet tomorrow or, for that matter, sometimes any food at all is enough to stimulate still another binge and another and another.

The one advantage the food addict does have over the drug or alcohol or tobacco addict is the motivating reward of slimness. At least he will look and feel good. But thinness is also something to be feared; I shall talk more about this later.

Like the other addicts, food addicts suffer

from withdrawal symptoms. They have both physical and psychological reactions when their "normal" food supply is in any way curtailed. These can vary from imperceptible to very severe symptoms. They are sometimes mistaken for other illness. There may be digestive, respiratory, urinary, circulatory, and emotional disturbances in any number of combinations. There may be constipation, diarrhea, heartburn, indigestion, gas pains, spasms, cramps, air swallowing, urinary retention, urinary frequency, irregular heartbeat, rapid heartbeat, chest pain, shortness of breath, itching, etc., etc., as well as depression, anxiety, irritability, fatigue, insomnia, excessive smoking, agitation, excessive worry, nightmares, unusual fears, etc., etc. Of course, the anticipation of these symptoms, let alone their onset, makes it most difficult to embark on a diet and initially to stay on one.

While most withdrawal symptoms, especially severe ones, occur at the beginning of food deprivation, they can also reoccur periodically even after dieting has gone on for a considerable length of time. Most of the physiological symptoms (as well as the psychological ones) are emotional in origin. As you will see later, food is highly symbolic. Deprivation of food and all that food symbolizes is felt as great emotional deprivation, which results in multitudinous withdrawal symptoms.

But by the same token, no amount of food can ever suffice, since these needs—for self-esteem, love, etc.—are never really mitigated or satisfied by food on any kind of realistic basis. This makes the addict feel hopeless indeed, as he continues to crave more and more of something—what, exactly, he doesn't know—that is supposed to be satisfied by food but isn't, which leads to the need for more food and more subsequent hopelessness.

People do not take well to pain, and this is especially true of obese people. It is, therefore, very difficult for them not to go back to immediate overeating as soon as withdrawal symptoms begin. Food addicts have a particularly poor frustration and anxiety tolerance. It is very difficult for them to put off immediate comfort, pleasure, or the alleviation of pain for long-term rewards.

The "rewards that may come later" seem especially vague to people who have a marked inability to "wait." Obese people score very poorly in the "patience" department. Eating is NOW—thinness is *months away* and only a vague "maybe" possibility. For all their imagination, the underlying hopelessness of obese people regarding any real or permanent change makes it very difficult to envision a state of thinness. Also, long years of practice makes rationalization easy ("Why suffer just now, it's been a hard week. So, I'll start dieting next month—after my vacation is over," etc., etc.) in order to avoid immediate food deprivation and withdrawal discomfort.

Food addiction complements and supplements lack of the EEF and MH, producing a vicious cycle from which it is very difficult to extricate oneself without considerable motivation and insight.

6

"I'VE BEEN THIN"

Thin thins don't make this statement, and they never allude to their current thin status either. They are nearly always thin, and they lack consciousness regarding their own weight for the past, the present, or the future. They *are* thin, and having once been thin is not part of their conscious concern.

Obese people make the statement, "I've been thin," over and over again because they invariably have a history of having been thin at one or another time in their lives. A loss of weight, followed by a short period of thinness, and then a regaining of it all—plus a few pounds—is nearly always part of the obesity profile. I have known fat people who went through the thin-fat cycle some twenty times in their lives. This includes one woman who fluctuated from really painful thinness (twenty pounds underweight) to severe fatness (over 100 pounds overweight). There are usually corollary statements, too, like, "I don't know, it just crept up on me and suddenly it was all there," or "Just went right back at it again—like a steam engine—eat eat eat, just couldn't stop."

What looks like a history of repeated victory and failure is actually no such thing at all. These cycles or phases are simply part and parcel of the obese profile in which insight and real control on a sustained level are utterly lacking. The thinning phase of the fat-thin cycle is just that—a passing phase, and on a realistic level should not be confused with permanency. Of course, doctors, therapists, and commercial weight-reduction groups often take undue credit for an obese person's weight loss when in fact they have only happened to "treat" him in his thinning phase—which inevitably passes on to a fat phase again.

There are very few exceptions to this cyclic occurrence, and these usually happen among people who are either utterly resigned to their fatness or have sufficient emotional insight and motivation to remain thin. Obese thins, for example, are going through the "thin phase," but they need much help in order to make this phase a sustained condition. How can any symptomatic condition disappear forever unless the underlying causes are effectively treated? In this connection, I want to say that many people do in fact "know" of the phase nature of the illness even before they experience it. I have seen any number of people—obese thins—who have nightmares about the return of the weight loss. Unfortunately, these too often turn out to be predictions of things to come.

Continual weight gain following loss almost always has a terribly demoralizing effect. Nobody likes to see very hard work go to ruin, however compelling the unconscious drive to ruin may be. The *loss-gain cycle* invariably produces much self-hate and hopelessness. Eventually, it often leads to abject resignation, which in large measure accounts for a weight gain exceeding the amount originally lost. Since fat people respond to self-hate and hopelessness with more eating, the obesity vicious cycle is further fed by this insidious process.

7

OBESITY = MISERY

A description of the obese profile would be incomplete indeed if we didn't mention the neurotic suffering of obese people. Obese people suffer much misery. Obese people are neurotic. Neurosis is a basis of obesity, which is the emotional state of mind leading to overeating. Obesity makes for more neurosis. Obese people—as long as they are without insight—remain overweight and fat.

Fatness, like all other aspects of neuroses, promotes impaired ways of relating to oneself, to others, and to one's work. Obese people are cut off from themselves and other people by the same psychology that produces a wall of fat. Obesity and overweight always have a destructive effect, both physically and psychologically.

Let us once again explode the myth of the "Jolly Fat Man." Fat people suffer repercussions in every conceivable department. They think poorly of themselves, and other people think poorly of them. Many people are prejudiced against them and openly regard them with contempt. More often than not, most people do not regard them as individuals at all. They become "You know—that fat guy" and even "That fat slob." Fat people are also extremely prone to every kind of physical degenerative disease, often leading to serious disablement and even death.

Well, how can obesity possibly enhance happiness? Of course it doesn't. In this, the last chapter on recognizing obesity, I want to state emphatically: Obesity Destroys Happiness! It Always Promotes Misery! Obese people are seldom jolly. If they appear to be jolly, this is usually a euphoric state that lasts a very short time and is a counterreaction to underlying misery. The fact is, obese people suffer from considerable depression. Sometimes the depression is quite evident. At other times it is just below the surface and is covered up by compulsive eating, which produces fatness and more depression. This is one of the main reasons some fat people become very depressed when they attempt serious dieting. Chronic underlying depression no longer compensated for by overeating then surfaces and is felt in its raw form, rather than in its more subtle manifestations.

Unfortunately, some fat people must live through their depression—on a fully aware and painful level—in order to get well. Depression is the result of self-hate. The fat man has much difficulty with anger and turns much of it on himself. He often overeats as a self-hating, self-destructive gesture. I will have more to say about the role of anger in obesity later on. Suffice here and now to say that obesity is the antithesis of happiness. Obesity in fact = misery.

PART II

UNDERSTANDING OBESITY AND THE FEAR OF BECOMING AND STAYING THIN

THE PSYCHODYNAMICS OF OBESITY

In the last part, I described the key signs and characteristics comprising the obesity profile. Now that we can recognize the obese man, let us go on to see how he got that way and what keeps him that way.

This section deals with the all-important psychodynamics of obesity. Understanding the origins and workings of the obese psychology is crucial to our purpose. We must understand the key factors that keep the condition going in order to exercise sustained control.

8

CONSCIOUS AND UNCONSCIOUS

There is much that goes on in the fat man of which he is unaware. All people have at least some unconscious or hidden feelings, memories, attitudes, driving forces, or motivations. This is particularly true of neurotic behavior, which is invariably due to hidden forces of which the individual has little or no awareness, let alone control. The more neurotic an individual is, the more he is subject to these tyrannical unconscious drives. Actually, the job of psychoanalytic treatment is to make the individual sufficiently aware of unconscious forces so that instead of being pushed about or compelled, he can consciously be his own boss and make choices and decisions regarding his own life.

Obesity is no exception. The fat man, unless insight liberates him, is the victim of a neurotic compulsion, is subject to hidden drives that dictate his overeating. Indeed, his eating compulsion is almost entirely generated and fed by motives of which he is unaware. He feels that he must eat but doesn't really know what is forcing him to do so since real appetite or ordinary metabolic need for food may be intirely lacking.

Like all neurotic compulsions, the overwhelming need to perform the ritual—here, overeating—can be extraordinarily powerful, overcoming all reasonable argument. I have an obese patient who recently made this too familiar, quite typical statement: "I didn't want to eat. I was sick—nauseous—but I had to go on and keep eating. I nearly ate myself into a stupor. Like something was driving me, but I don't know what." She was, in fact, driving herself, of course, but doing so with neurotic needs and a neurotic rationale that she was not in touch with.

Another very important statement made by a patient is the following: "I want to lose weight, I really do, but at the same time it's almost like I really don't want to at all, like there's something about it that scares me." Yes, on a conscious level she really does want to lose weight. But unconsciously, there is much that goes on in her that in fact wants to sustain her weight and is in fact afraid of thinness. She wants to be thin, but for reasons unknown to her she is afraid of being thin and is therefore compelled to overeat, thus guaranteeing her fatness. This compulsion—largely unconscious—comprises the psychology of obesity. As we go on, we will understand more and more about this psychology, as well as about *the fear of thinness*—both of which are largely unconscious in the fat man's scheme of things.

Conscious awareness—insight—is the most important key to eventual liberation. Yet, it is not easy to make that which is unconscious, conscious. As a matter of fact an individual will exert considerable resistance to "not see what gives." This is largely so because he has little desire to go through the painful struggle, re-evaluation, change, and growth that awareness may bring. It is very difficult to give up old, familiar beliefs, habits, "comfortable" ways of relating— however sick they may be—for unfamiliar, new but initially "uncomfortable" ways of relating. People are afraid of the unfamiliar, and this is particularly true of insecure people. Keeping things unconscious, out of awareness, is an excellent way of preventing the threat of change. Increasing conscious awareness is the first step toward change, and taking this first step requires considerable motivation.

9

BEGINNINGS

Of course, all creatures have an innate desire and drive to food and eating. An infant born without this "instinct" could not survive. Some experts believe that many fat people are born with an exaggerated food drive or mouth orientation. Others believe that some obese people inherit a predisposition to remain fixed at the infantile mouth- or orally-oriented stage of development. I feel that some people may indeed have a greater biological development, sensitivity, need, and response in the mouth area. But I'm also convinced that not all of them develop an obese state of mind or ever become fat. I'm also convinced that many obese people have a problem, the roots of which are discernible in other than the inherited or biological area.

In the many obese patients I have seen in consultation, as well as those I have had in treatment, it soon becomes apparent that food played an unusually large role in their early lives. When the proper questions are asked, we soon learn that the family food and eating history of the obese person is decidedly different from that of true thins. There is very often a family food pattern that has been there from birth. In most cases it has been there before the birth of the obese person in question, since it has been handed down from generation to generation. Many, many, obese people were, as children, subject to households where there was a great food preoccupation and where huge amounts of food were served. Many of them have no idea at all as to what constitutes "normal portions."

In my own case it wasn't until I left my parents' home that I realized "other people" didn't eat ten or twelve lamb chops, three baked potatoes, three other vegetables, and plenty of bread, as the main course, among equally voluminous courses as a normal dinner. This kind of three-meal day was further supplemented by nearly unlimited snacks, including malteds, milk and cake, peanut butter sandwiches, and so on. Of course, there was a plentitude of every kind of candy available at all times—enough to rival any sweetshop. I really thought that everybody ate this way unless of course they were sick or very poor.

Unfortunately, many obese people share this kind of early background. Along with huge portions, they are also *encouraged* to eat; taught that food is the solution to most problems; that special foods are rewards for special performance; that an enormous appetite is synonymous with good health; that fatness (in children) enhances looks, personality, and general attractiveness. Some of this is "taught" and "learned" on an almost blatant level. Much is a matter of subtle but steady unconscious conditioning.

The growing infant and child is extremely perceptive of and receptive to what goes on about him. Without being aware of it, he is busily absorbing and imitating those close to him. Much of this "food conditioning" takes place on an unconscious level. And, precisely because it is deeply ingrained in his young developing unconscious, he will be greatly influenced by this conditioning in his food outlook all of his life. Because of the various "unusual" familial attitudes toward food and eating, food will take on special symbolic significance, as I shall describe in the next chapter.

There are people who escape obesity despite the fact that they have come from obesogenic, or obesity-producing, households. But these are households that are particularly healthy in all other respects. These are households that provide an environment that, despite its gluttonous outlook, is favorable to the development of much emotional health in growing children. This kind of household is exceedingly rare, however. Generations of obese families are *largely* made up of obese people.

Obese people are neurotic and almost always produce neurotic environments—part and parcel of which is the obese climate. Children who are subject to excessive permissiveness, overprotection, uncaring parents, emotional deprivation, vindictiveness, favoritism, inappropriate behavior, inconsistencies, rejection, and other pressures that produce poor self-esteem and insecurity will develop neurotic behavior. Their general functioning and performance in their work and in their relationships will suffer. Those children who are subject to a neurosis-producing environment that is also obese will end in their neurotic development to include manifestations of obesity.

Neuroses are, after all, the many aberrated ways people learn (through imitation and testing or trying out) to behave, in order to cope with insecurity and anxiety. Obesity is one form or part of neurotic behavior. The obese person eats to allay his anxiety, which in no way gets to the roots of his anxiety. As a matter of fact, overeating and fatness make him more anxious and more ravenous, thus completing a vicious cycle. To conclude: Physical and hereditary predisposition may or may not exist, but a neurotic and obese subculture and family environment is nearly always evident in the genesis of obesity.

10

WHEN FOOD IS NOT FOOD

To thin thins, food is food and nothing more than food, however delicious, enjoyable, elegantly served, or charming the company at the dinner table may be.

To obese people, food is much more than the everyday sustenance we call food. It has symbolic connotations that play a very important role in their lives. Symbols play a very important role in all of our lives. The meanings and representations of many symbols are buried in the unconscious. Very often the symbol becomes more important than the object it originally represented. For the obese man, food is a highly symbolic object. As a symbol, it usually has a combination of meanings or representations. The same is true of the process of eating, including chewing, swallowing, and assimilating.

These symbolic representations spring up

neither suddenly nor casually. They develop insidiously, slowly, subtly, and almost completely unconsciously over a period of years commencing with infancy. The future obese man, as a child, has no idea that he is being conditioned to see and feel food as other than food. He is unaware that he is, in effect, being brainwashed, and those around him are unaware that they are doing it to him. The obese man is similarly unaware that feelings about food have also spread to feelings about the process of eating. Even years later he may be unconscious of the fact that eating and food have very special meanings for him.

Very often, the degree of emotional sickness is directly proportional to the degree of symbolization. The more disturbed the individual has become over the years, the more symbolic and bizarre food and eating representations tend to become. Food-oriented parents unwittingly *reward* their children with food (sweets); *punish* their children with food (withdrawing sweets); *admire* their children with food ("That's a good boy, you eat so well."); *frighten* their children with food ("If you don't eat enough, you'll get sick." "Not enough vitamins and you'll get TB." "Not enough milk, your teeth will fall out."); *teach* their children with food ("If you have two apples . . ." "So there was a rich man who had lots of nice things and a refrigerator with all the food you could eat."); and so on.

They do all this directly, indirectly by example and innuendo, and they do more, too. Their own mouths become the centers of emotional expression, and not only with voice or words but also with how they eat. They eat angrily. They eat gently. They eat sweetly. They eat dourly. They eat ravenously and indiscriminately, banging dishes and the refrigerator door in one mood, and then eat only sweets—delicately but steadily—in another mood. They don't know that they are demonstrating feelings through food and eating. Their children don't consciously know or form verbal thoughts about these correlated food/feelings either. But deep down where it counts, where it is all stored, the children observe all, learn it all, and the formation of symbols for a lifetime takes place.

So we meet obese people who see and feel food as love, warmth, comfort, security, reward, stimulation, sedation, sex, and many other things. We see people who are *angry eaters,* who unconsciously choose to eat huge quantities of hard, "tough" foods that they can bite and tear apart in a rage until the anger dissipates. We see people who are so terrified of their anger that they don't dare to eat tough foods lest their anger show. They invariably choose soft, mushy foods that require little energy and in no way can be linked to hard, emotional, angry chewing. Then there are the "love seekers," who have come to cherish sweet foods rather than sweet, potentially loving people.

Many obese people see getting fat as both a symbolic and concrete way of keeping a layer of fat between themselves and other people. They know very well that most people will shy away from a serious relationship with a fat man, so fatness becomes a way of sustaining physical and emotional distance. Many people eat in order to become grotesque and sick as a form of self-punishment and self-hate. There are people who seek exotic, "different" foods rather than chance different experiences or relationships with different people.

For many people, individual foods have unconsciously taken on special meanings. When they feel particularly inadequate, they will gravitate to one particular food; when happy, to another one, and so on. I had one patient who always had an uncontrollable urge for chocolate after eating pastrami. He couldn't understand this strange appetite combination until he recalled that his mother invariably rewarded him with one or the other whenever he was a "particularly good boy." He had no understanding of his compulsion until it became apparent in treatment that he combined both—"rewarding" himself with pastrami and chocolate—each time he completed a particularly good business deal. It soon became apparent that he always got "uncontrollably hungry" after "any kind of victory." His mother had been dead for years, but her influence lived on. Eventually, we both learned that his wife was very food oriented, too, and that without awareness they had both already food oriented their two young children to a significant degree.

For many obese people, the taking in and

assimilation of food has a common but special symbolic significance. The whole process of ingestion and assimilation is felt as a substance-adding device—a form of self-aggrandizement. This is very often a compensation for feeling inadequate, incomplete, for lacking anything in any way. Food is then seen as the general replacement for these inadequacies and as a comprehensive solution to all problems, especially those of "feeling small" in any way.

Sometimes it is almost as concrete and simple as just that. I had one patient of relatively small stature who weighed 350 pounds. After many months of analytic work, he realized that he was attempting to make up in width what he lacked in height. He also felt that excess weight gave him a feeling of being more substantial (of more substance), of being "stronger," of being "more important," of being "more masculine." These unconscious feelings about what food and excess weight symbolized precluded his getting thin until they became thoroughly conscious. He could then look at them and cope with their obvious irrationality. He next went on to examine and resolve his real problems, which had been covered for years by fat. He was able to see that no amount of food or weight made him feel *really* adequate. Once able to see and tackle the origins and feelings of his inadequacy, he was further able to see how fatness, seemingly giving immediate relief, actually contributed to further feelings of inadequacy. Thus, he was able to cope with real issues rather than symbolic representations. He became thin and happier, too.

People who do not develop this kind of insight go on eating because ultimately, despite symbol representation, food is food and it is not love, warmth, adequacy, or resolutions to problems. The fat man goes on craving whatever he needs because, despite its symbolic illusion, food and eating provide none of it. If anything, it invariably complicates and heightens his real needs, despite the illusion of momentary comfort that it may bring. This is largely why the fat man is always hungry. He chronically hungers for entities unrelated to food the symbol.

11

THE OBESITY MATRIX

All people are neurotic to at least a certain degree. The more neurotic we are, the more our function is impaired. To the extent that we are cut off from our feelings, anesthetized as it were; to the extent that we behave in rigid, codified ways (in response to inner tyrannies not at once apparent); to the extent that we have lost the ability to behave spontaneously (spontaneity is impaired by loss of contact with our feelings, from whence spontaneity springs), we are neurotic. Neurotic behavior often results in symptoms like overt phobias (unreasonable fears), compulsions (having to perform a particular ritual over and over again for some unapparent, unconscious reason), psychosomatic manifestations, overeating, etc. These symptoms are also defenses against anxiety. They are a way of at least temporarily mitigating or escaping anxiety. I'll have more to say about anxiety in the next chapter.

Since we are all neurotic to a certain extent, we all have at least some emotional difficulties in common. Many books have been written about neurotic character structure. For the purpose of our work here, I want to describe some important aspects of obese neurotic character structure. Obesity is after all part and parcel of a whole *psychological matrix,* some aspects of which are also found in non-obese people.

Obese people are unique, however, by virtue of their obesity, overeating, and fatness, as well as by the consistent pattern of character traits that they nearly all present. They are not usually aware of this psychological matrix, which remains unconscious but which to a very large extent dictates the behavior of the individual, especially in the ways he relates to himself and others. Of course, there are exceptions and individual differences. Obese people, like all other people, have much health as well as sickness. Varying combinations of health and sickness and countless inherited characteristics, as well as differences in environment and experiences, will result in variations of behavior. But we do find a certain few personality characterological traits consistently present again and again in obese people.

I call this combination of personality characteristics *The Obesity Matrix.* The obesity profile described the outward signs and symptoms of the condition. The matrix is not nearly as apparent, but proof of its existence does not require too much digging by the experienced examiner. There is no hard line between the profile and the matrix, just as there is no concrete boundary between the unconscious and conscious. They sort of flow up and back and merge here and there. But for the most part, it is the hidden matrix that sustains the overt profile.

The obese man, like the very young infant, is extremely dependent. His emotional dependency parallels the infant's physical (and emotional) dependency. He finds it extremely difficult to manage on his own, and he therefore seeks to attach himself to a partner who will provide emotional sustenance. If the obese man seems to be functioning well and even on an independent level, investigation soon reveals that he has a "good mama" at home who provides strength. The obese man operates much like the small boy who swaggers down the street seemingly able to care for himself among his fellows as long as he knows that his mother is at home ready to support his every need.

This dependency relationship may be hidden by cover-up surface phenomena. I have known a large number of seemingly "strong" obese men who were married to seemingly self-effacing, compliant, "weak" women. Investigation, however, proved otherwise. Despite surface bluster and a wife's intent to make her husband "feel strong," the relatively self-generating, more flexible, real source of strength in the family turned out to be the "weak" partners (crisis situations are good test grounds).

As long as he sustains a going relationship with a "dependable" partner, the obese man may function on some borderline, satisfactory level and even seem strong. When this emotional umbilical cord is cut, he will often become blatantly anxious, severely depressed, and unable to get along in any capacity at all, until a new mother-substitute relationship is established. Thus, often without awareness, the fat man clings to the emotional breast.

Very often his wife (or a substitute—his mother, girlfriend, sister, or male friend as well) unconsciously responds by concretizing his need—plying him with food as a symbolic substitute for mother's milk and emotional support. More often than not, both partners are consciously unaware of the reality scene. They do not know that theirs is, in large part, a parent-child relationship, or that one partner in a way contributes to the other's fatness. Confrontation will, if anything, bring denial. The wife or substitute does not want to face, let alone disturb or give up, her powerful role of "mother of a man." Thus, she helps sustain his emotional dependency and fatness.

The obese man finds it almost impossible to cut the emotional umbilical cord since he suffers severe reactions to emotional deprivation. Of course, he finds it very difficult to be alone or to function in a solitary capacity. Food is often his only connection to home and a reminder of his partner; and in this connection, when he is alone, eating is even more common than usual.

This overwhelming need for "someone" will produce a considerable drive in the "love" department. But the love he seeks is very special. Ideally—and he seeks a neurotic ideal—it will be bestowed by a partner who anticipates his every need, who sustains and strengthens his every move, who supports his every gesture, and who ideally lets him in on none of this lest it hurt his pride. In short, he seeks the ever-embracing, all-warming, all-protecting, instantly self-sacrificing "love" of the "ideal, good mama." The obese woman seeks the same in a father substitute.

Neurotic people do seek and find each other, satisfying efforts to complement and supplement neurotic needs. But this kind of "love-dependency" quest remains largely unconscious and is covered by a veneer of romance and mutually attractive characteristics. The attraction of sick factors does not negate the effect of healthy ones, too. Of course, neurotic ideals do not exist and, of course, this kind of sustenance-sucking relating has little to do with the responsible give-and-take relating that takes place between emotionally well-developed adults.

Obese people find less than "perfect" love partners and bitter disappointments: abused feelings; disturbed sexual patterns reflecting disturbed relationships (here, too, they have impossible expectations); and frustration. Temper tantrums, depression, anxiety, and hysteria are also not uncommon. Things get particularly stormy when a formerly dependable partner becomes somewhat healthier and makes moves to emancipate herself and develop her own individual needs, values, and identity.

As with most neurotic people, obese people are terribly concerned with being liked and being admired. To a man who basically feels insecure, inadequate, and exceedingly vulnerable in a potentially hostile, threatening world, love and admiration seem like the only means of securing safety. However, the need for everybody's love and admiration makes it most difficult to be oneself, to express one's feelings—especially angry ones—and generally to assert oneself. This kind of anticipation of inner censorship and curtailment of feelings makes an individual much less effective in all of his endeavors, thus ultimately contributing to greater feelings of inadequacy and, in the case of the obese person, to more eating.

The obese man or woman will very often

present a picture of gregarious, ebullient,
expansive charm that will sometimes border
on grandiose and even manic behavior. He
will seem to see the world through rose-
colored glasses. His expressions will be
exaggerated and his speech full of
superlatives. He will act like a grand, gestur-
ing circus master. At times he will play the
part of an irreverent clown. Sadly, un-
derneath it all, more than anything else he
would like to be taken seriously. More than
anything else he really craves respect, largely
to compensate for his enormous lack of self-
respect. Unfortunately, fatness adds other
people's prejudice and self-contempt to his
own.

His outgoing, expansive behavior is largely an enormous cover-up and reaction to
strong feelings of childish, petulant, angry
inadequacy. While the obese man, like other
troubled people, may in fact have many fine
assets—good humor, intelligence, talent,
etc.—he will unfortunately feel no solid
sense of ownership of any of them. Similarly,
he does not have a solid, realistic knowledge
of his limitations. This lack of realistic
evaluations of assets and limitations makes
for inappropriate appetites and wide mood
swings. The obese man often requires the
grand gesture to give him an immediate,
however temporary, sense of adequacy. He
largely acts to win over people whose love
and admiration he desperately requires.
Love and admiration seem to him to com-
prise the emotional food that will compensate for his lack of self-esteem, as well as

his very real, however hidden, self-hate and potential depression. An abundance of this "emotional food" makes the world seem safer to him.

Too often, though, each time he feels rejected and hurt, "emotional food" is immediately converted into "oral food," which he takes in in huge amounts. Rejections and hurts that a healthier person may take with relative equanimity are often enough to send the obese man into massive self-destructive eating binges in an attempt to allay deep depression.

Swinging between feeling inadequate and feeling grandiose, the obese man often undervalues himself and just as often overrates his capacity and ability. This makes gross errors in judgment common. Having had this experience of poor judgment and bad decisions, he sometimes develops much inhibition about making any judgment at all. This often applies to dieting: "Oh, I can lose forty or fifty pounds very quickly any time I decide." Failure from poor evaluation and judgment increases an already over-burdened storehouse of self-hate, cynicism, hopelessness, and resignation.

The obese man is not a flexible man. He is rigid, feels brittle, and is afraid of unfamiliar, untested ways. He clings to the familiar, not feeling sufficiently strong to tackle new roads, let alone face potential deprivation. He is afraid to deprive himself of anything—especially food and all that it symbolizes for him—because he still feels like the clinging, vulnerable infant who cannot long sustain life without attendant sustenance. The obese man feels that he has little or no reserves of emotional strength and therefore must always be at a ready and quick source of friendship, love, admiration, and food should succor suddenly be needed.

Of course, overeating and consequent fatness—often to the point of grotesqueness—contribute further to his internal emotional difficulties and his relationships with other people. The entire syndrome of neurotic difficulty and fatness becomes a fixed habit that is very difficult to break in an inflexible man terrified of change.

Sometimes, however, the outside world impinges on the fat man and despite himself, he is faced with the need for change. This may come under the stimulus of the death of a close one or undue failure or undue success. Some obese men, depending on the degree and availability of healthy aspects of their lives, will rally to their own standard and move in the direction of change and health. Others will, in severe fright, shun people altogether in favor of food, having completely given up and abjectly surrendered to their sickness.

12

ANXIETY, CONFLICT, AND FRUSTRATION

These three bedfellows play a very important role in the obese man's life. This is especially true because his tolerance to them is so poor.

Nobody is exempt from anxiety, conflict, and frustration. They are very much part of the human condition. There are inevitably times when we all feel nervous, tense, and fearful without apparent cause, when to our conscious minds we seem to be inappropriately upset and apprehensive. Anxiety, if well tolerated, brings on a minimum of symptoms (defenses against anxiety). If poorly tolerated, anxiety will itself produce any number of symptoms, which are designed to help the individual feel less anxious but which, in fact, create greater anxiety, thus producing a snowballing effect.

The symptoms or escapes or defenses that anxiety brings on are of both the physical and the emotional or psychological varieties. These may include headache, disturbed vision, high blood pressure, irregular heartbeat, digestive disturbance, skin rashes, asthmatic attack, and so on, as well as voracious and exotic appetite, attacks of panic and hysteria, insomnia, depression, hypochondriasis, phobias, compulsions, inhibitions, peculiar and inappropriate ritualistic behavior, strange beliefs, delusions and hallucinations, and so on.

Unavoidably, there are times when we are conflicted—torn in two directions at the same time—when decision comes only after great struggle and sometimes seems almost impossible. There are always times when for one or another reason we cannot have what we want, when we are not blessed with rewards that we feel ought to be forthcoming, rewards that may be entirely justified and completely expected, when normal, natural, appropriate desires and appetites cannot, for one or another reason, be fulfilled. In short, we are disappointed and frustrated.

To the extent that we are basically insecure and infantile, we will respond to conflict and frustration with more anxiety, contributing still further to the snowball effect. Tiny infants can't understand disappointment or frustration. When they cry, they want their bottles; they can't wait. They do not understand that the bottle comes from somewhere outside of themselves where time-consuming complications can take place. They feel that breasts and bottles are part of themselves and are turned on and off as needed. A delay is regarded in much the same way as a stuffed nose is when air is needed. It takes time for the infant to learn where he ends and the rest of the world begins—to get over his "megalomania," part of which many adults retain forever.

People who are particularly neurotic and lacking in self-esteem will have very poor ability to struggle through conflict in order to establish real values: where they stand on various issues, their attitudes and feelings about themselves and the rest of the world, and so on. They will also find struggle in conflict for the purpose of making meaningful decisions very difficult. Their frustration tolerance will be minimal. As I indicated in the last chapter, the obese man has exceedingly poor self-esteem and sense of self. He finds conflict and struggle very difficult and therefore has a very vague sense of his real values. Since values are the cornerstone of self or a sure sense of identity, his sense of identity is very shaky. This contributes further to feelings of fragility, making him particularly prone to attacks of anxiety, which he tolerates poorly.

We know that the obese man still operates with many unconscious residuals from infancy. Therefore, like the infant, he finds frustration, disappointment, and waiting very difficult. He feels these as exaggerated hurts and undeserved punishment. As with most children, waiting is felt as an exquisite teasing, a kind of torture, and as with children it is very difficult for him to do today for tomorrow's promised rewards. Since most of life's endeavors require at least some patience, the obese man feels further frustrated and anxious in his need for immediate gratification.

Usually, the one thing he can get at once—take in and immediately feel as an added strengthening substance to his shaky feelings of self—is food. In a sense, it operates like mother's milk in the infant and, here taking on much symbolic value, gives him an immediate sense of security, however false or fleeting that sense may be. In short, the obese man responds to most situations and especially to conflict and frustration and to waiting (unfortunately, realistic dieting to lose weight requires much waiting) by generating a great deal of anxiety, which he tolerates poorly.

One of the principal symptoms of anxiety in the obese man is eating and more eating and still more eating, which, from a psychiatric viewpoint, is a defensive attempt to allay or relieve anxiety. In conflict, in frustration, in anxiety, or in anticipation of potential anxiety, the obese man eats. If his anxiety is severe enough so that it carries over into sleep, spilling into dreams too revealing for comfort, he will wake during the night in order to eat.

Night eating is evidence of much anxiety, particularly poor tolerance for anxiety, and much self-rejection and self-hate. It is almost invariably a sign of a more than ordinarily well-entrenched and complicated obesity problem requiring professional help. The night eater wakes and eats because he cannot face himself or his problems even during the sleep and dream state. Relief is sought via "food reward," "food love," "food ego substance," as well as through the dissipation of energy and anger through chewing. In addition, a state of fatness or overweight is sought in order to maintain an entrenched status quo. I shall describe this extremely important phenomenon or dynamic later on.

As with many neurotic defenses against anxiety (phobias, compulsions, delusions), some quick relief may take place because of the symbolic significance of eating and food, and also because the person is diverted from his actual problems. Relief is never sustained, however. Problems, neurotic attitudes, confused feelings, unresolved conflicts, self-contempt, and disturbed relationships remain intact and become even more entrenched and complicated. Fatness produces still more self-hate, self-doubt, greater hopelessness, resignation and cynicism, and still greater problems in relating to other people. This inevitably leads to more frustration, more conflict, and more anxiety. Thus a vicious cycle is created. The obese man is trapped in the anxiety food cycle from which it is almost impossible to extricate himself without considerable motivation and the help of insight.

13

ANGER AND APPETITE

When I am asked what is the single most prevalent but hidden characteristic of obese people—a universal but unseen obese dynamic that is ever present—I have no trouble at all in answering immediately: *Anger!*

Obese people seldom seem or look angry. Many of them manage to smile and to even look jovial in what ordinarily would be anger-provoking situations. Obese people are very often not conscious of feelings of anger. In circumstances where other people would immediately feel and readily show anger, obese people will usually seem perfectly content with no evidence at all of irritation, let alone anger. *But* obese people are invariably very angry people, and obese people *always* have great problems with their angry feelings. All people who have emotional difficulties, that is people who have problems with relating to themselves and others, have "angry problems."

The culture we live in willy nilly imposes its will on all of us. This takes place through films, books, and other forms of art, and school, constant personal contact with each other and with the conventions and ideas of generations past. Our culture, unfortunately, inherits and sustains some very inhuman and unrealistic dicta and pressures. Among them is its attitude toward anger. Implications and direct pressures are consistently promoted that define anger in any form as uncivilized, disrespectful, immature, and generally dangerous and sinful. Children are brought up in "sick emotional climates" where they are taught (by word and example) that they are not entitled to feel anger freely, let alone express it. Of course, attempted obliteration of a normal, natural, human emotion is at least as disastrous as attempting to do away with the blood supply to a limb. One leads to physical gangrene and the other to emotional gangrene.

Despite these pressures, relatively emotionally healthy people are still able to retain enough freedom to feel and to express anger warmly and constructively. This helps promote honest and improved communications, making relationships healthier and more fruitful. Equally importantly, it helps free an individual to experience all of his feelings—particularly love, warmth, and a sense of beauty (not blocked by a corrosive storehouse of repressed anger)—and adds immeasurably to the development of a real sense of self, of identity, and of healthy independence.

People who suffer from emotional difficulties (since all of us do, this is only a question of degree) are particularly susceptible to the pressures of cultural or environmental irrationalities. These combine with familial and inner pressures to effect emotional paralysis, crippled self-esteem, creative atrophy, and relating difficulties. People who have problems with anger invariably suffer repercussions in all areas. The inability to allow oneself to feel and to express anger also causes aberrations of all other feelings. People who repress anger must develop a storehouse of angry feelings, which produce all kinds of "poisons," including anxiety, psychosomatic illness, depression, abused feelings, hypochondriasis, and so on.

Obese people, in terms of the obese matrix, having inordinate dependency needs, the need to be liked, and the need to be admired, have great difficulty with anger. They know and feel very little about the expression of healthy, warm anger as a way of conveying displeasure—as a means of clearing the air—and improving relationships. Anger represents a threat to dependency relationships. It represents a change of status quo and the possibility of incurring wrath and being "disliked." Obese people are particularly prone to repressing angry feelings and under sweet smiles and layers of fat invariably have a huge storehouse of repressed rage. Any possible leakage of angry feelings makes them extremely anxious and, as described in the last chapter, they respond to anxiety with more anxiety and a whole myriad of neurotic symptoms—especially overeating.

Overeating is the single most effective and ultimately destructive symptom of the obese defense system. Obese people both repress and express anger by eating. Food is the enemy as well as the ally in angry rages. They attack the food in lieu of the object of anger. They eat and store food to feel stronger and to push down and hold down anger. This almost always takes place on a totally unconscious level. The obese person, confronted with a blatantly anger-provoking situation, does not know that he is "attacking" his food or engorging himself for support against the weakened state he experiences when there is a threat of anger coming up in him. He does not know that he is having an anger attack or a temper tantrum. At most, he thinks that he feels particularly hungry and is having an attack of appetite. He has no real feeling knowledge that he is using food to quell angry feelings, which, if they leaked through to awareness, might make him very anxious. He has no idea that he uses food and fatness as an inert paralyzing block to the possible seepage of anger.

We all may know people who actually eat themselves into a stupor as a form of anesthesia. There is hardly an obese patient whom I have treated who has not eaten in rage. When confronted with anger and appetite connection, they will either deny or accept the explanation but they will not make the connection on a deep and emotional level for months. They can only do this after they have developed a greater capacity and tolerance for anxiety, frustration, and anger.

Working through anger problems to a healthier ability to feel and express anger is one of the most important areas in the *realistic* treatment of obesity. It is most rewarding to see the fat come off as anger is loosened and expressed. As the fat comes off, the obese person comes into touch with more and more of his long-accumulated anger, which gradually dissipates along with his overeating. This is one of the reasons why dieting obese people are often temporarily angry. In addition to giving up the illusionary support of highly symbolic food, they are also giving up a prime defense against anger and are losing and melting the accumulated, solid block of anger of a lifetime. Their feelings are beginning to flow freely.

As I mentioned earlier, depression is due to anger turned inward on oneself as a form of punishment. In a depressed, angry rage at himself, the obese man is capable of eating unto death. Since he often does not dare to express anger at others, he frequently turns anger at others inward on himself, contributing further to his feelings of depression. Angry fat people also use their overeating and subsequent fatness to keep a distance between themselves and other people. While they need dependent closeness, they are also afraid of anger coming through. They neither wish to express anger to others nor do they wish to chance the anger of

others. Thus, some angry isolationists unconsciously maintain a repulsively fat
physical state to ward off the possibility of
human involvement and the possibility of
anger.

Fatness is, of course, also used as a
surreptitious weapon. I have had more than
one obese patient who knew that her
husband found fatness sexually repulsive.
She unconsciously "got even with him" by
getting even fatter than she ordinarily was,
each time she got angry at him. It took many
months before she realized that she even got
angry, let alone that her periodic eating
attacks were temper tantrums and a form of
sexual revenge. Real emotional insight made
for vast improvement in her marital life and
particularly in the sexual area.

Obese people almost always have sexual
problems. The combination of grotesque
fatness and repressed hostility are very
destructive to closeness and good sexual
relating. As anger dissipates in obese people
and, with it, *fat,* relations eventually im-
prove. (I say eventually; initially they may
become more complicated, as I will explain a
little later on.) As with all people, improved
relations always include the ability of friends
to feel and to express anger warmly and
openly so that reparation and further
growth can take place.

14

IMAGES

We all have conglomerate unconscious and conscious feelings about ourselves that are sometimes called images. Thus, we have an image consisting of how we feel about ourselves; an image of how we feel and think other people feel about us and see us; an image of aspirations or how we feel we would like to be; an image of how we feel we would like other people to see us. Some of us have a split image: one part consisting of so called "good points" and the other of "bad points." All of us have a physical image of ourselves—that is, how we see ourselves in our mind's eye—what we think and feel we look like.

These images may be partially conscious, but the larger part of them remains unconscious throughout an entire lifetime. In effect, each image represents and is the result of the individual's entire psychology and his entire history, including his neurotic and healthy development, all of his assets and liabilities, and all of his feelings and attitudes. These images begin to form very early in life and though some small changes or modifications may occur, the images are extremely well developed, solidified, and resistant to change by the time adulthood is reached.

These images are extremely important because in very large measure the ways we feel about ourselves, want to be, want to seem to others, etc., dictate our ways of relating, our choice of work, partners, and attitudes, and very nearly our whole lifestyle.

The closer these images are to reality, the more realistic and appropriate our behavior will be. The further removed they are from reality, the more inappropriate our behavior will be. Bizarre images (formed originally because of bizarre and difficult backgrounds and having roots in much sickness) will produce a lifetime of bizarre functioning. To cite an extreme, a man who sees himself as the Emperor Napoleon will behave in a way appropriate to that image but most peculiarly in the context of reality. To cite a more common (and less sick) case, a woman who sees herself as saintly may not overtly act "peculiarly" but she may be doing herself chronic harm by being terribly constricted about angry feelings and self-assertion and by being unable to say *no*, and so forth. In time, the dictates of her saintlike image may convert her to an emotional timebomb.

Our various images are the result of each other and function interdependently. This is particularly true of the physical or visual image—*the way we think we look*—and its corollary, what we think other people see when they look at us. Few people bring

much objectivity to this perception. Few
people know how they look or for that matter how anybody else really looks. Their vision is clouded by their own image of
themselves, by the image they project onto
others, and by their particular needs. I have
known women, very homely by any
standard, who saw themselves as beautiful
because they could not otherwise go on. I
have had a number of patients who, upon
feeling better, felt "better looking," and they
looked better too as tension left their faces.

But there are distortions—and there are
distortions. If an individual chronically feels a
great deal of self-hate, this almost always
affects the physical view he has of himself. I
recall a beautiful actress (more noted for her
exquisite features than her acting) I saw in
consultation who was convinced that she was
ugly. Because she could not stand "the ugly
sight of myself," she removed all mirrors
from her walls. This was highly symbolic of
how contemptuously she felt about herself
in all areas. She was completely convinced
that she had fooled everyone with makeup—that she was really ugly—although she
actually used a minimum of cosmetics. Her
delusion was the result and reflection of
enormous self-hate and chronic depression.
No amount of public adulation about her
great beauty mitigated her *physical visual
image* one iota since it was in no way based on
real books.

I have also known people who were homely children but who turned out to be very
good-looking as adults. Some who felt

generally good about themselves appreciated and accepted the change. Others with less self-esteem developed an image of ugliness based on ungainly childhood looks that was in no way modified by the obvious changes that had taken place.

As described in previous chapters—particularly in The Obesity Matrix — obese people are neurotic people, and the various conglomerates of feelings or images they have of themselves are invariably quite distorted. A great many have a totally unconscious combined image of saintliness and omnipotence. Attempts to fulfill the divergent requirements of both at the same time produce much inner conflict and anxiety with its rampant repercussions. Failures to fulfill the impossible, combined requirements of both roles (martyrdom and mastery) make them feel that they constantly "fall short," which produces strong feelings of worthlessness and self-hate.

The physical visual image is extremely important in the obese emotional scheme of things (obese psychodynamics). Since how obese people think they look will in large measure determine how they want to look—often, unfortunately, engendering much hopelessness since the discrepancy will often seem too large to bridge—this image and eating will have very intimate connections. In keeping with a neurotic outlook and obese status, the obese man and woman, much to their detriment, will be much more concerned with the pressures of vanity than with those of health needs or even possible death.

Unfortunately, this physical image in obese people is nearly always unusually distorted. Recent experiments, in which formerly fat people chose what they thought were their proper silhouette outlines or dimensions, indicated that they consistently chose outdated measurements regardless of present reality. Very thin people continued to draw outlines of very fat people. On the other hand, I have had patients who see themselves as thin even though they are more than 100 pounds overweight. A man I know used to look in the mirror at a big roll of fat he supported around his waist for years convinced that it really was a "band of muscles covered by a thin layer of fat."

One woman I know who had compulsively become severely underweight (she actually looked like a concentration-camp victim) was convinced that she could not fit into any normal-size chair. She came to see me because her internist feared that she was developing a severe inability to eat that might possibly result in her death from malnutrition. She still saw herself as fat, and no degree of thinness could dislodge her feelings and vision of this image. Another man I know constantly bought clothes, including shoes, that were literally large enough to fit a man at least twice his size. One woman I knew always had black and blue marks on her arms and legs. Though she was enormous (420 pounds), she still saw herself as thin and constantly bumped into things—judging her size and necessary clearing space by image rather than by actuality.

Another woman who was very fat and quite grotesque had beautiful eyes, hands, and feet, and these were her image of herself. She had only three dresses but literally hundreds of pairs of gloves, shoes, and every conceivable kind of nail polish and eye makeup. When asked to draw her own picture, she drew hands, feet, and eyes—nothing else—leaving blank paper in between. In her visual image she managed to block out her self-hating fatness.

There is a trap or double-bind situation that comes up as a facet of the distorted image again and again. It goes like this: The obese man has an image of himself as a thin boy. Connected with this "boyishness" are feelings of vulnerability, inadequacy, and weakness. Though he hates his fatness and himself with it, he sees his added weight as extra substance and protection against feeling as he did when he was young, thin, and "weak." Thus fatness, while it may be revolting to him, may at the same time come to represent strength and adult masculinity. Thus he is caught in a double bind: He hates himself for being fat but doesn't dare get thin lest he encounter feelings of inadequacy associated with things in his past life.

As with all of us, obese people tend to become self-hating when they don't measure up to aspirations. With obese people this is particularly true of aspirations about dieting and becoming svelte. In their magical way of looking at things, which I describe in the next chapter, they would like to lose all the necessary weight in an hour or two at the most. They feel there must be some magical formula for weight loss that constantly eludes them, causing more hopelessness, resignation, and self-hate.

As part of the obese image, there is often enormous unconscious vanity. The individual aspires to be the most beautiful person in the world. Anything less than this exalted status is seen as sheer ugliness. Thus, self-hate and resignation follow and lead to wild abandon in eating, the feeling being, "If I can't be the most beautiful, I may as well be the ugliest." Fat here covers up vanity and also promotes the image of potential great beauty—like the student who protests his belief in his genius, "If I studied, I could have gotten 100 percent." The fat woman, in effect, can go on believing in her great beauty and all of its wondrous effects—"If I would only diet." Since she does not diet, she takes no risk with confrontation of reality—less than perfect beauty—and thus wards off self-hate. If confronted with the fact that she is indeed vain, she will say, "How ridiculous, just look at me. Would anybody who is vain let herself get this way?"

Many obese people have an extremely fixed fat image, in addition to well-entrenched feelings of lack of lovability and general lack of self-esteem. This distorted physical image is most resistant, most firmly entrenched, and almost impossible to dislodge or to even modify. This is not as hopeless as it may sound because (as I will describe in the last part) with knowledge, healthy control can be effected even without change of image.

This image and these feelings have roots in early insecure backgrounds and are also fed by the feeling that "no one can really love a fat man." This feeling is not helped by much cultural prejudice against fat people, which the fat man himself also believes: "They're lazy," "fat and stupid," etc. Many people believe that fat men look like women and are sexually incompetent and impotent. Though fatness may bestow a soft feminine look, it does not cause sexual aberrations or impotence. If the fat man becomes more active sexually upon losing weight, this is largely due to increased feelings of confidence and attractiveness.

Often, perfectly normal thinness, arrived at after painful and heroic dieting, brings on bitter disappointment because the obese thin still feels fat, unlovable, and full of self-contempt. This is so because his various images—how he feels about himself (in all things) and particularly his physical image (how he sees himself in his unconscious mind)—have not changed at all. Yes, the image can and most often does remain untouched even when body dimensions have actually changed. This discrepancy (between feelings emanating from the image the actual sight of one's body) brings on disappointment, bitterness, self-hate, hopelessness, anxiety—and then new onslaughts of eating, new stores of fat, and resignation.

With awareness and knowledge of the image and of the feelings of discrepancy and disappointment and inappropriate expectations, this need not happen. By making the unconscious conscious through insight the individual must come to realize that loss of fatness simply does not resolve all problems. The obese thin can then exert sufficient control so as to remain thin even if his image of himself does not change remarkably.

15

MAGIC

Obese magic, a myriad of psychological defenses, is secret stuff. Obese people keep their magical beliefs from themselves and others, but like all unconscious ideas, magic permeates a good deal of their feelings and actions. In this chapter I simply want to give away some of these secrets.

Obese people, like many of their true-thin neurotic confreres, believe that life and happiness is simply a matter of finding some kind of elusive panacea that solves all problems. This panacea may come in the form of an all-perfect, all-giving lover. It may come in the form of vast riches. It may come in the form of enormous, never-ending glory, which may be derived from any number of fantastic positions or circumstances. It may come in the form of a great surge of willpower and mastery, which will enable the possessor to overcome any problem with sheer force.

Untold riches do exist, but they seldom resolve basic problems in relating and often produce great disappointment. Riches (contrary to unconscious magical belief) do not ward off death, do not produce longevity, and do not produce happiness. Millionaires are sometimes also fat—and unhappy. Perfect lovers, perfect love, and saintly, "perfectly dependable," devoted partners do not exist. If they did, they too would resolve nothing and would not effect growth.

Glory brings on a need for more glory, and like food it is at most only momentarily satisfying. Utter control and mastery dissolve like sugar in water in a world that, by its very nature, is utterly unpredictable. Willpower, however great, has never willed anybody out of an emotional problem or a mental hospital. It never takes the place of *insight.* But magic has little to do with reason or reality. The need for magical belief goes on as long as the individual has a need to evade healthy responsibility and confrontation with reality.

The obese person says in effect, "Love me, love my fat." Even though he inwardly feels ugly, his magic also permits him, at the same time, to demand that "true love" overlook his grotesque appearance and see him as magically attractive. Failure to see him as other than fat and repulsive is seen as a lack of acceptance, a lack of love, and as a rejecting affront. It takes much magic to reconcile feelings of ugliness with demands for assurance of attractiveness. But the obese man and woman have ample magic to make this and other irrational discrepancies possible.

To the obese person, magic makes *now* become *forever* so that what cannot be accomplished immediately feels as if it cannot be accomplished at all. You can readily see how this makes dieting, which requires time, very difficult. If one is *fat* now, then it feels like fatness is of necessity a forever state. But at the same time, magic (not intruded upon by the exigencies and limitations of reality) makes the obese person feel that he does have forever—that time and life are endless. This makes him feel that *one day* he will lose weight. *One day* he will really solve his problems. *One day* he will grow up. *One day* he will wake up and really start to live. It is just a question of the right time. Thus, somehow in this regard— perhaps as the result of inertia or resignation rather than from real patience—he feels he can wait and wait for that day to arrive because he has all the time in the world. This may be so even though he has already reached an advanced age, as well as having the deterioration in health so characteristic of the obese state.

Obese magic strongly colors the obese man's feelings about his health and longevity. He feels magically immune and somehow protected from the onslaught of diseases that affect others. Despite evidence, proof, and even personal tragedy, he always feels that high blood pressure, coronary occlusion, paralytic strokes, early death, and so on are really reserved for other fat men. They simply are not meant for him. However many warnings he gets through symptoms or from his doctor, he will go on overeating and really feel that he will somehow magically escape the dreadful effects of fatness on health and life.

Some obese people have the magical belief that they themselves are in no way responsible for their fatness. It is other people who make them fat. It is the fact that there is too much food around. If there were only fewer social events. If their wives wouldn't cook so well so that food smells so good. While these may or may not be contributing factors, the core of the problem lies within the fat man himself, but he would rather focus on *outside* sources of trouble.

Food, and its highly symbolic significance, as well as weight and thinness, have all kinds of confused magical connotations. Feelings about food can change from moment to moment, and diverse feelings can magically exist at the same time. Thus, food is seen as poison—the enemy—and also as the realization of all its symbolic representation—warmth, protection, added self, love, and more.

Thinness is seen as the possibility of metamorphosis. It is thus terribly threatening (I shall go into this all important dynamic in the last chapter of this part), but at the same time thinness is seen as the cureall and endall of the obese person's problems. Since the basic problems don't end with thinness, the state of thinness without insight brings bitter disappointment, a back-to-eating movement, and fatness.

(Even insight, unfortunately, does not end all problems. As long as we are alive we have problems. Having problems is part of the human condition and of being alive. Insight does not end the generation of problems, but it does help to resolve them effectively if they do occur).

The obese man periodically—and magically—thinks that he is "cured." He thinks that he has been metamorphized into a true thin. This often happens halfway through a weight-losing diet. He suddenly believes that he has developed temptation tolerance that he either never had or that is likely to be poorly developed at best. He will suddenly bring home cake, pie, ice cream, and other "poison" foods for the "rest of the family" and will insist on going to restaurants notorious for serving very rich foods.

Of course, his magic will not prevail. He has no temptation tolerance and will succumb, sometimes ruining his diet permanently. I say permanently because the obese man often operates in an all-or-nothing fashion. Once he breaks his diet he will tend to continue to break it all the way rather than go back to it and resume.

There are many other magical ideas and beliefs, some of them highly individual. Some obese people erroneously believe in the magic of exercise, in the magic of "concentration," "hypnosis," "faith healing," "oversexualizing," and so on. But before I close this chapter, I want to mention a particularly destructive and prevalent form of magic. Many obese people, in their need for emotional support and magical belief, endanger their lives by going to all kinds of quacks and by taking all kinds of pills. I have known any number of people who sought and followed the advice of absolute charlatans because their own reputable doctors refused to participate in "magic cures." I know obese people who have tried all kinds of dangerous "food fads" as well as completely phony "spiritual help" in an effort to find magic rather than reality. Pills, even when used judiciously, rob the patient of a sense of participating responsibility, which is all important in sustaining weight loss. The fact is that the only magic possible is emotional growth arrived at through struggle, increased insight and self-awareness, real interest in self-preservation, and resolution of basic problems, which leads to increased self-esteem.

16

THE FAMILY FAT CENTER OF ATTENTION (FFCA)

In various books I have repeatedly stated that people are afraid of change or unfamiliarity and will struggle valiantly to maintain *familiar* status quo situations. This clinging to the familiar, however sick or painful it may be, is particularly applicable to the family of the fat man (or woman) and to the fat man in relation to his family.

Families also have their unconscious images. These consist of the family members' conglomerate feelings about themselves and each other, as well as the patterns in which they relate to each other. Though he is often unaware of it, each family member usually plays out a "role" relative to other members of the family. Very often, there is the family "wise man," "family infant," the "family spinster," "family success," and so forth.

Sometimes there is the "family fat man," or what I call the *FFCA—The Family Fat Center of Attention.* Above all, fatness brings attention. This is in the form of pity, contempt, ridicule, prodding, salesmanship, pleading ("Please please go on a diet"), caring, and so on, but it is all attention. By virtue of obvious dimension alone, the fat man or

woman calls attention to a "family tragedy."
In a perverse way he adds to the family position of prestige through martyrdom. This is
a family with a problem. This problem is
often discussed outside as well as within the
confines of the immediate family. In this way
the fat person becomes a kind of conversation piece.

He also becomes the externalized object of
other people's problems. He is used by them
as an excuse for their problems. They also
concentrate on his obvious problem to keep
away from and dilute their own. Some people will surreptitiously tempt and overfeed
the fat man as a way of satisfying their own
appetite while avoiding food themselves—a
kind of eating through identification—thus
having one's cake and eating it too. They also
make themselves feel better by comparing
their lot to that of "that poor fat sister" or by
actually venting spleen by contemptuous
attacks on the fat relative.

The fat man not only puts up with this, but
usually also clings to this *familiar situation*
just as the whole family does. But the fat
man does so for reasons additional to the
force of familiarity. Remember that we are
dealing with a relatively dependent, fragile-
feeling individual. It is not easy for a person
like this to stand up to both his neurosis and
that of his family in order to make a constructive move. The family may claim that
they want him to get thin, *but* on an unconscious level they want no such thing at all and
they will sabotage his every effort.

This is not so strange when we consider

their need to sustain him in his familiar "conversation piece" role as the "family fat center of attention." For example, a cake is brought into the house at a crucial time in dieting by a "loving wife" or family members will tell the fat man that he is beginning to look pale and wan after he's lost ten percent of the load he has to lose. None of this is accidental, and of course it presents tremendous resistance to a possible change of image in the family constellation.

But, there is in this connection still another very important factor. I call it the *PIP* or *Privileged Invalid Position.* Because of his *fatness,* the obese man often retains the role of invalid. He can use this role in several ways, all unconscious for the most part. He can feel crippled and martyred and on this basis demand care and fulfillment of dependency needs. As the "family freak" he can fulfill narcissistic needs by getting attention. By thrusting his invalided, grotesque self on his family, he can embarrass them, make them feel guilty, and thus surreptitiously discharge anger and "get even." Giving up the *PIP* is particularly hard for people who make many claims on the basis of it: "You owe me this and that because I'm not as lucky as you are. I'm sick. If you don't believe it, just look at me."

I am reminded of one woman who had no idea that there was anything at all in the family order of things that kept her fat until she had a memory that loosened a whole stream of insightful associations. She remembered for the first time in twenty-five

years that as a very young child her father
used to bounce her on his lap and say, "My
sweet little fat, roly-roly-poly girl." Twenty-
five years later, much heavier and much
older, she was still attempting to be a kind of
dehumanized love object. This went on as it
so often does, despite the fact that she no
longer lived in her father's house and now
had children of her own. Seeing her parents
occasionally had sufficient effect because,
like most of us, her family constellation and
demands were well rooted in her unconscious and needed minimal stimulation to be
activated. Eventually, she realized that she
was "stuffed" as a child and that without
awareness she was stuffing her own children
and attempting to stuff her husband as well,
in an attempt to continue a sick but familiar
state of affairs. It took much work and
struggling for her to break through the
resistance both she and her family put in the
way of possible change.

Here, too, there is often a very powerful
doublebind situation in operation. It goes
like this: "We will have contempt for you if
you stay fat because you embarrass us. But
we will take away attention and 'love.'"
There are relatives who are actually happy
with the beginning of the fat man's weight
loss but who become more and more
irritated and sullen as he continues to lose
weight and change his status quo. This has
been reported to me time and again by un-
comprehending dieting fat people. Sometimes, as with wives and husbands of
alcoholics, a mate does not want to give up

the position of "invalid protector" that makes her or him feel useful and prestigious. Even though he swears he wants a "cure" for the victim and on one level he really does, he hates it if his "invalid" gets thin because it will upset the family balance and threaten familiar patterns. The dependent person unconsciously "knows" what is happening and feels torn and helpless indeed when this outside ambivalence is added to his own difficulty. A powerful ally in the form of psychiatric support and insight is sometimes needed to stand up to a "loving family's" peculiar form of resistance and destructive influence.

17

GLUE AND CEMENT AND THE
MATTRESS EFFECT

In an effort to find relief from conflict, confusion, and anxiety, people unconsciously cut themselves off from their own feelings, attempting to produce an anesthetizing effect. They also cut themselves off from involvement with other people as well as from interests and activities. The kinds of *cutting off* vary in degree, but they always have a destructive effect on aliveness and spontaneity; on creativity; on the possibility of fruitful and happy relating; and, in short, on functioning in any area.

The obese man is no stranger to this kind of "defense activity." But much of his kind of cutting off takes place via his state of fatness. He uses food, overeating, and fat as a substitute, a cover-up, and a suppressor of feelings. For him, food and the complete concentration on food and eating often take the place of people. There is a complete emotional investment in food, leaving little or no emotional energy for people, even though perfunctory motions are made in their direction.

I have known a number of fat people who prefer to eat in solitude. This involves more than embarrassment over amounts eaten. It is a form of withdrawal from people. It is also a displaced form of sexualization—to fat people there is much sensuality in their eating and much dissipation of the sexual feelings that usually take place in private in our culture.

But the fat man also uses his fatness to present a nonthreatening, noninvolving, nonidentifiable, bland, amorphous, anonymous glob-like surface to the outside world. All fat people tend to look alike since fat obliterates distinguishable features. I call this the "mattress effect." Shaped like a cushioned mattress, the fat man or woman says in effect: "Say what you will, do what you will, it all simply bounces off of me. I have a layer of fat to hide behind. You cannot get to know the real me. I stay buried beneath my jovial bouncy mattress and you bounce off it without ever getting to know me, let alone ever being able to hurt me. All you see and know is a jolly fat man because I don't get involved with you at all."

But the fatness and the whole eating compulsion that sustains it does something else too. I call it the "cement and glue effect." Fat is the glue that keeps the entire neurotic structure—including the fat man's family position—cemented in place. It serves as an impenetrable neurotic envelope, keeping a delicate but fixed neurotic balance in place so that neither turbulence nor growth (healthy development of self) takes place. Fatness, in this way, represents enormous resignation, keeping the individual in fixed position. His energy is spent eating and accumulating more glue so as to further cement his resignation from real living and to further enhance his surrender to neurosis.

In short, food and fatness is the obese man's major means of preventing an iota of movement in the direction of healthy struggle and the real resolution of problems. In effect he sits back and hides behind the façade of being "fat, dumb, and happy." Unfortunately, he is fat, lacking in insight, feels terribly frightened of giving up his fat status, and is very unhappy.

18

THE FEAR OF BECOMING
AND STAYING THIN

For the obese person, becoming and staying thin is at one and the same time a most attractive possibility and a potentially horrendous experience. On the one hand, he overinvests the thin state of being, seeing it as the certain resolution of all problems, as well as the realization of a myriad of unrealistic, magical, utopian possibilities. On the other hand, he is deathly afraid of becoming thin and unconsciously develops a severe phobic response to that possibility.

This desire but also this fear of thinness engenders strong ambivalent feelings and produces severe conflict and anxiety, making "getting thin" an unconsciously very fearful possibility. Yes, the obese man has a special phobia peculiar to the obese state of mind. He is phobic to thinness and dieting. This is, in effect, a *comprehensive fear or phobia* in that it includes and represents all of his unconscious fears and all of the issues in his life that he has been unable to face.

As the converse to fatness—"the big cover-up"—thinness represents "the big exposure" and confrontation with multitudinous fears, painful memories, unresolved conflicts, irritating conditions, and hitherto rejected hidden feelings, including anger, jealousy, envy, possessiveness, sexual desires, feelings of injustice, of having been abused, and still others. In short, it represents the antidote to fatness: It is the solvent that melts the glue keeping everything that might create anxiety "safely tucked away."

The obese man does not know that the items safely tucked away in the repressed state have an autonomy of their own or that they do great damage. He does not know that exposure is finally the only means of attaining real freedom—because it ultimately resolves situations and because it means that one is consciously in charge of all parts of himself. The blackmailing effect of areas he cannot face *will no longer* be there.

I have seen any number of people who have asked, "How can I so resist getting thin when I really want it so badly?" These people show considerable understanding inasmuch as they know that they do in fact "resist" thinness. They do not know, however, that they are truly very fearful of becoming thin. Later on, with increased but still incomplete insight, some say, "I would like to become thin but I don't want to change anything else about myself." Here they are demonstrating that thinness does in fact represent change. They do not know that it does not represent horrendous change. They do not know that the realistic changes that it will bring with it are not utopian but are nonetheless gratifying. They, like most neurotic people, eventually find out that symptoms (such as depression, phobias, etc.) cannot disappear on a sustained basis without basic changes and resolutions of problems. They eventually find out that they do in fact have the strength, health, and wherewithal to make the necessary adaptations to the non-exaggerated, actual changes that do take place with thinness.

Thinness also represents a change of status quo on both a personal and familial level. For a resigned fat man, any change represents unfamiliarity and the need for growth and adaptation, both of which are felt as very threatening. The fat man or woman once thin can change, in a healthy direction, slowly and tolerably. But obese people don't see it this way. They feel that thinness will necessitate many changes, and that people around them, and they themselves, will expect and demand *immediate* changes in all areas of living. This belief will be fed by the imagined exaggerated rewards of thinness that the fat man has always nourished.

His fears will be further fed by actual changes in his environment as soon as he becomes thin. Since the family will be threatened with a loss of the family fat center of attention, they will become irritated and attempt to sabotage his effort, even though they may ostensibly act pleased. They may also remind him of eventual loss of his *PIP* (Privileged Invalid Position). There may very well be statements like: "Now that you are getting thin, no reason to hang around the house. Go out and meet people and have a good time."

So thinness represents exposure of painful areas, changes in personal positions, changes in family patterns, giving up other defenses and illness, encountering a certain degree of anxiety, and, in general, *change.* Change, in turn, represents turbulence and chaos and in fragile individuals stirs up considerable self-doubt and hopelessness. I knew one patient who, it turned out, was afraid to become thin because "it would make my father happy." Eventually the following situation became clear. Her mother was not an attractive woman but my patient had a beautiful face. She was afraid of becoming thin because with a beautiful face and figure her father would find her more attractive than her mother. (This was also a deeply hidden desire on her part.) Since she would "show her mother up," she would lose her mother's much-needed love, the entire family balance would be destroyed, and there would be utter chaos and confusion. None of these feelings were apparent on the surface. Much work was necessary to uncover these issues and to resolve them.

Another of my patients was terribly fearful of any kind of sexual contact. She saw thinness as "enforced sexual contact." "My family would then force me to go out and would expect me to meet someone. This way they don't bother me. Being fat I can be sexless—neither man nor woman—I don't have to do anything."

I have had at least several patients, men and women both, who were unhappily married but who were afraid to admit this source of unhappiness to themselves. Despite the fact that they found much fault with their mates, they were also terribly dependent on them and fearful of upsetting the status quo. Interestingly, analysis revealed that they saw thinness as conferring immediate beauty and irresistible sex appeal that would absolutely necessitate involvement with people other than their mates. They preferred to keep this probability and temptation as distant as possible lest the whole marriage applecart become upset.

Thinness in this peculiar way became the fearful loss of a much-needed crutch—their wives or husbands. Since these people harbored so much hopelessness, it took much work before they could entertain the possibility that exposure of marital difficulties could lead to improvement in their marital state rather than its termination. It is fascinating to note how this belief and the exposure and resolution of "hidden" and repressed problems can initiate serious dieting and a sustained move toward thinness.

It is likewise extremely gratifying to watch an ameliorative double-action take place. As the fears that thinness represents are exposed and resolved, fatness dissolves. As fatness dissolves, more and more of the problems and fears are exposed and resolved. It is almost as if the disappearance

of every few pounds and layers of fat
permits more and more of oneself to come to
light; as the glue gets unstuck, greater emotional health and freedom of movement take
place.

Part III

OVERCOMING OBESITY
AND THE FEAR OF BECOMING
AND STAYING THIN

CONTROLLING THE CONDITION

This part deals with the application of our information to the problem. In the following chapters, we want to convert our information to remedial means. It is crucial that we move toward a realistic outlook in our understanding of obesity. This will enable us to succeed in effecting sustained and even permanent control over obesity's monstrous child: overweight or fatness. The "emotional mechanics" of dieting can then be applied rationally and effectively.

19

"I'M SICK"

A person who is chronically ill *but* does not know it will not seek help and therefore will not get well. This is particularly applicable to the obese person, with whom confusion and unrealistic denial of sickness are commonplace.

Let us approach this initial phase of the problem in several steps.

1. We must be absolutely convinced that obesity is a neurotic condition, an emotional sickness that, if uncontrolled, periodically produces overweight or fatness, a physical sickness. Obesity is a sickness of malignant magnitude in terms of destruction: emotionally—especially in terms of pain and suffering—socially, and functionally (all areas of function including the economic); physically (contributing to all degenerative diseases and destroying longevity); in terms of the deleterious effect on *all* areas of one's life.

Yet many obese people have great resistance to embracing this belief because they are unwilling to take this first step toward giving up an old familiar way of life. Well, make no mistake: This is the first step, and it must not be skipped over. It is imperative that we understand and accept the fact that *obesity is sickness*—an emotional sickness or neurotic state of mind, call it what you will *but* understand that the obese man or woman is *sick*.

2. As with all sickness, we must ascertain the diagnosis. We now know that obesity is a sickness and now we have to admit whether or not we suffer from this sickness. There is an excellent chance that the answer is *yes*; otherwise you probably would not be reading this book, unless of course you are reading it to help someone else in whom you are interested. Making this admission, if you approach the possibility with any degree of openness, is not difficult. You simply have to apply the criteria of the obese profile. The unmistakable signs and symptoms are all there. *But* it is much more difficult to admit having the illness than to accept it. By acceptance I mean acceptance without self-hate and also without rationalization: "I just have it a little bit; other people have it worse."

If you've got it, you've got it! You cannot be a little obese any more than you can be a little pregnant. If you have this sickness, then you must admit it, own up to it, and get involved in understanding it—that is, if you realistically want to do something about it. This also means feeling responsible (not guilty, for guilt stands in the way of adult responsibility) for having participated in the illness and taking responsibility for participating in its control. You cannot begin to get well if you believe that someone else is making you sick, however much they may realistically contribute to your sickness. You cannot begin to get well if you wait for someone else to stop making you sick. You will not begin to get well if you wait for someone else to make the diagnosis. *You must make the diagnosis!* As with alcoholics, no real improvement will take place unless you own up to the fact that *you* are *personally* sick. However distasteful, whatever resistance you feel, you now know that there is a sickness called obesity and you must now admit that you suffer from this sickness.

3. The next step is understanding the illness. You cannot hope for improvement by being a passive observer or even a "passive participant." This is not appendicitis where you lie down on a table and the surgeon does all the work. Obesity is a chronic condition that will require controlling for a lifetime, and this is simply not possible without personal interest, involvement, and understanding.

To understand the dynamics I have discussed is not difficult, but it is very important. It is a jumping-off place, a beginning toward opening up and understanding more and more dynamics. As with all areas of human behavior, the entire picture is never complete, but I am sure that you can contribute your experience and understanding to further elucidate this chronic syndrome.

4. The next step involves understanding *our own personal* dynamics, characteristics,

peculiarities, symbols (especially food symbols), and vulnerable areas. Neurosis almost always has stultifying, individuality-killing effects. Since it destroys individual spontaneity, it substitutes rigidified, codified ways of behavior. Therefore, it is not really surprising that neurotic people very often behave similarly. As they get well and shuck off the common shackles of rigidified neurotic behavior, they can once again tap individual resources and develop, acting in a free, individual, differentiated manner. This, of course, is also true of obese people and that is why it is possible to draw a fairly accurate account of obese neurotic dynamics (the obese matrix).

But even in neurosis, individual differences will exist. We each have different genetic structures, different environments, histories, assets, liabilities, and limitations. The more we know about ourselves—and especially about ourselves vis-à-vis obese dynamics—the better equipped we will be to tackle the job. For example, it is very valuable to know what situations usually make us anxious or angry or bored, and so forth. Which people have what effect? How do we respond in particular situations? I will go into this topic of "sensitive areas" at greater length a little later on. Suffice here to say that active participation in assessing and understanding your *own* reactions toward obesity is very important.

I want only to say here that insight directed toward the understanding of oneself is invaluable. I shall speak of psychiatric help later on. However, it is important to note that it is the psychiatrist's job to understand the patient only so that he can help the patient understand himself. Yes, the patient—you—must actively participate in understanding more and more of how you *personally* operate with obesity in the light of your ever-increasing knowledge of obese dynamics.

5. It is important to develop the realization that changes need not be made immediately upon becoming thin. Indeed, they cannot be made that quickly. It is best that changes in social habits, dressing, going out, attitudes and demands on oneself be made slowly—and compassionately. In fact, they are best made before beginning to lose weight and continued throughout the weight-losing phase as gradual preparation for thinness. Realization that thinness does not mean that one has to immediately cast himself into unfamiliar areas is extremely important in mitigating the fear of thinness. Ideally, change and the development of tolerance for unfamiliar areas, which really constitute healthy growth, will go on for the rest of our lives and long after our desired weight goal has been achieved.

20

CURE AND CONTROL

Chronic illnesses—diabetes, rheumatic fever, arteriosclerosis, neurosis, for example—are never completely cured. Few illnesses are ever completely eradicated. Residuals always remain. However, many chronic illnesses can be arrested and controlled so that relatively healthy, painless, comfortable functioning can be reinstated.

Obesity, however, is incurable! I feel very strongly about this fact, and even more strongly about the necessity for the obese person to understand, absorb, and digest this fact in much the same way that the alcoholic must realize that his alcoholism can never be "cured." Because of the chronic nature and pervasiveness of obesity and especially because of the implacable, fixed, ultra-resistant nature of the images, the obese frame of mind can never be totally eradicated. But obesity can be understood and insight can be established, so that the malignant effects of the condition can be arrested and even turned back.

Even more important, although the obese mental state cannot be cured, it *can be changed.* Through the illumination of insight, its effects can be diminished and thus obesity *can be controlled.* When the various forces involved work surreptitiously, unconsciously, and autonomously, we are victims of these forces and there is nothing we can do but obey the compulsions they generate. When, through insight, these forces are brought to light, we can then be in charge and establish healthy central control, breaking the need for mechanical, compulsive, ritualistic behavior. Thus, *we can control and even completely eradicate* the compulsion to overeat. Although we cannot cure obesity, we can understand it enough to *cure* our phobia or fear of becoming thin and we can sustain thinness so as to cure—or let us say destroy—overweight or fatness.

It is extremely important to know that obesity is controllable but incurable. Our position, as I mentioned, is similar to that of the controlled alcoholic. As I explained earlier, however, the alcoholic has the advantage of being able to live without alcohol. We cannot live without food and, since total cure is not possible, food for us will never quite lose either its symbolic or addictive value. Therefore, as much as we learn about situations that are dangerous for us (that produce eating attacks) and particular personal symbolic values of food and the dynamics of addiction, we must never consider ourselves "cured" lest we become grandiose and vulnerable. *Knowing* that we are arrested addicts will make us cautious and effective. The only alcoholics who "succeed" are those who realize that they are never cured. The same effective realization applies to us.

One of the things the obese person must learn both intellectually and also as a very part of his conditioning and of himself is an understanding about food portion sizes. Since he does not have an EEF, he can only compensate for this lack with knowledge, thoroughly learned through training. This intellectual knowing how much is enough to eat is the only way he can possibly ever cope with his mouth hunger. Of course, the strength of this learning and training will be particularly critical when he is, for any reason, particularly vulnerable. I shall talk about "vunerables" in the next chapter. Also, since we know, *really* know, that we are not cured and since we *never* fool ourselves on that score, we will not suffer devastating disappointments. Even though we know that we have poor temptation-tolerance and ought to avoid excruciatingly delicious temptations, we also know that there will be times when we will succumb.

"Uncured" people, however well they are managing, will encounter bumps in the road and periodically will fall back on old ways. But we will be prepared by the knowledge of our noncured vulnerability. If we know that we are not cured, we also know that we will at times have "old-time attacks." When these attacks occur, we will not be disappointed and thus there will not be recriminations and the generation of much self-hate, self-doubt, and hopelessness, which lead to massive chronic attacks and destruction. On the contrary, knowledge of incurability and anticipation of difficulty will make such attacks highly limited and infrequent, so that the state of thinness will not be at all impaired. It is true that we will never be *true thins,* but we can be realistic and happy *obese thins* for the rest of our lives—and only we need know the difference.

21

VULNERABLES

I use the term *vulnerables* or *sensitive areas* to designate any time, circumstance, place, or person that the obese person will respond to with an increased level of sensitivity, feelings of fragility, and vulnerability. These are the areas that will produce anxiety, to which the obese man will have a history of overeating responses. It is invaluable to know when we are anxious and vulnerable. We don't always know this and are especially blind to our anxiety and vulnerability if overeating covers up our recognition before it even begins. Knowing our "vulnerables" is particularly useful. It gives us the opportunity to avoid them if we can and if we so choose (there are times when we don't feel strong enough to confront anxiety-producing situations). It also gives us an opportunity to be on guard in anticipation of the urge to overeat.

Thus, we can begin to take steps to break the anxiety/food reaction-habit cycle. Some of the following are very common obese vulnerables: Periods of unusual excitement, aggravation, changes (of job, home, school, friends), physical sickness, boredom, parties, pregnancy, premenstrual periods, aloneness, loneliness, sexual excitement, any frustration, break-up of relationships, news of tragedy, unusual success or joy, examinations or any period of pressure, fatigue, overwork, contact with threatening people, contact with *anger-provoking people,* celebrations, being in restaurants, and many other situations.

I had a patient who always went on an eating binge a few hours after a certain cousin called her. It took some time before she made the connection. As it turned out, she had strong hidden feelings of competition, jealousy, and envy that this cousin stimulated. Another woman went on eating binges whenever her husband came home more than an hour late. Eventually she realized that she saw his lateness as her lack of lovability and as a rejection from him. One man I know binged every time he had to go to a family function. Another man binged whenever the stock market went down (responding almost in mercurial inverse ratio to the Dow Jones index). An older woman I know binged every other week and it took some time before she revealed to her-

self and to me that this was in response to
sexual advances by her husband, which
occurred with biweekly regularity. It is always valuable to review the events of the
hours and days immediately preceding a
binge. Trying to remember back and
associate to how you were feeling and thinking can be revealing and valuable. It is constructive to look at a binge as a chance to
extend insight rather than as an opportunity
for self-hate, which leads to more and even
chronic binging.

While some vulnerables can be quite obvious, others can be completely hidden and
very difficult to ferret out. Of course, it is
extremely helpful if we are alert to the
possibility of vulnerability. Each of us will
always find that we do in fact have at least
several individual vulnerables to which we
react with great consistency. With work and
insight we may even be able to rid ourselves
of some of these vulnerables. But this cannot
happen if they remain buried and unconscious so that we don't know what they are.

It is often helpful to work backward. Let
us say you feel like eating, even though you
have already eaten plenty for the day. Instead of eating, you try to arrive at what it is
you are really feeling. In other words, what
would *food the symbol* be giving you at this
time? Is food love, a tranquilizer, a
stimulant—what? If you know, you can trace
back to the area of vulnerability.

Let me give you an example. A man I
knew always overate at about 11 P.M. when he
watched television after a hard day's

work. He stopped eating, but he felt anxious and traced back his anxiety. He realized that his food urge came at a time of great fatigue—that food represented energy and stimulation and that his vulnerables here were depletion of energy and fatigue.

A young woman came to realize that she had an urge to binge whenever she got "a longing feeling." By the process of free association, it soon developed that food filled that longing feeling. It further developed that food to her was always symbolic of love and acceptance. Eventually, it became apparent that she longed for *food love* each time she longed for love, which occurred whenever more than two weeks went by without a date. For this particular girl, being dateless for two weeks was the fixed and hitherto unconscious criterion for loss of popularity, rejection, and loss of self-esteem. As symbols and vulnerables take on meaning—as they are revealed—much about how we relate and function, in general, will become clearer. Patterns of behavior and repeated habitual reactions will emerge. If we can withstand anxiety a little bit (and this ability to withstand anxiety will increase) and do some detective work, we will be rewarded with more and more knowledge of our symbols, our vulnerables, and our ways of responding. This will result in increased ability to sustain control.

22

TO STRUGGLE

There are struggles and there are *struggles.* I absolutely do not advocate struggle for struggle's sake; that is, for the sake of self-imposed pain and martyrdom. But I know very well that constructive change will not take place unless we struggle. We are interested in struggling, in issues that will produce greater growth and health. This kind of struggle does in time get to be easier, more frequent, and more constructive. For our purpose, here are some areas of struggle that are particularly worthwhile:

1. To struggle to withstand anxiety long enough to be able to trace the source of the anxiety. The tranquilizing effect of food obliterates this pathway to insight. It also robs us of the possibility of getting increasingly accustomed to withstanding anxiety. This adaptation to anxiety prevents the snowballing effect of anxiety producing more anxiety. It helps us to break the anxiety-overeating response cycle. Therefore, when we feel strongly urged to *eat,* it will more than pay off to try and hold off, even if that means feeling quite anxious. It will be even more rewarding as we learn to find the source of our anxiety.

2. To struggle against self-hate, hopelessness, and guilt each time a binge occurs. These attacks on oneself can only have a demoralizing, weakening effect and invariably destroy self-esteem and anxiety-tolerance, thus promoting further binging.

3. To struggle to develop a greater fund of "self-information," especially about our own particular food and eating symbols and our own vulnerables and how they fit into our ways of behaving.

4. To struggle to accept ourselves even when we find out things about ourselves that we'd rather not face. We are all of us, at times, jealous, envious, less than generous, and have other unpleasant aspects to our natures.

5. To struggle to be kinder to ourselves: To be able to say, "*No,* I don't want that." To struggle to be able to say, "*Yes,* I want this or that for myself."

6. To struggle against one's own and one's family's resistance to change in the status quo. To take a chance on unfamiliarity—unfamiliar feelings, places, ways of relating, and people.

7. To struggle to accept angry feelings and to express angry feelings warmly and humanly so as to prevent the self-corrosive effects of stored-up rage.

8. To struggle and take a chance on thinness, that extraordinary glue solvent. As thinness occurs and fat disappears, emotional revelations and emotional growth can take place.

9. To struggle to *Take the Big Chance*—en-

tering the mainstream of the world of the living, as a real identity, unprotected by an envelope of fat. This includes buying clothes, testing your taste in things, socializing. For some people this may be very difficult at first. But this kind of struggling improves self-esteem and makes ensuing struggling interesting, welcome, and even more constructive.

23

"I CAN'T DO IT MYSELF"

Many people *cannot* do it by themselves. They try and try, but after many years of trying it becomes apparent that they need outside help. Unfortunately, many people would rather cater to sick pride than to real self-interest. They are more concerned with what "other people will say" than in getting much-needed help. Those people often go to an early grave—fat. What about outside help? *Caveat emptor!* Charlatanry and chicanery abound, and the "weight-reducing business" has attracted many ruthless, totally ignorant "operators."

I feel that any decent diet works and that the only way to lose weight is to diet proper-ly. The best diet is one commensurate with your physical status. This should be determined *only* by your internist or family doctor. No diet should commence without thorough medical consultation and evaluation. Pills and pill pushers are destructive in that they rob you of active participation in a process that cannot be sustained successfully without your active participation and sense of responsibility. You must know and feel and it must be a fact that *you are doing it* and not a pill of any kind.

Except for a minute number of people who suffer from glandular disturbance, which will be discovered by competent medical examination, chronically fat people are *obese.* Obesity is not a disease curable by diets nor a physical or physiological disease. It is an emotional disorder, a neurotic constellation, *a psychiatric problem.* Strict medical intervention does not remarkably ameliorate psychiatric conditions even when the medical man is a highly competent person. Nonmedical charlatans, of course, can do great harm in treating psychiatric conditions whether their help comes in the form of quack machines, quack massages, quack chemical steam vapors, or the indiscriminate use of drug mélanges. These usually consist of combined diuretics, heart stimulants, energizers, tranquilizers and metabolic hormones. Without benefit of great expertise they can be deadly—especially to the already anxious person.

Some of the weight-reducing groups, commercial and noncommercial, are very successful in the losing-weight phase of the cycle. The mutual support of people with common problems, identifying with and getting encouragement from people who already show progress, the pep talks and interest of allies can all be very effective, especially with suggestible people.

But it is easier to lose weight than to sustain the weight loss. The former is dramatic and demonstrable and for the moment serves as a focal point removed from the many real problems. The latter throws one back on oneself in a continuous confrontation with the dreaded thin state and all that it implies. Weight-reducing groups cannot hope for sustained weight-loss success unless there is accompanying work on underlying obese dynamics so that the fear of becoming and staying thin can be combatted. I feel that it is safer for people to enter these groups only after qualified psychiatric consultation takes place. Fortunately, the worst that usually happens is a weight loss and then a gain and discouragement. But, in an unusually fragile person, the loss of a major defense, the loss of a great percentage of one's body weight and substance (the juxtaposition of their new state of thinness to their old image of fatness) often produces very severe psychiatric complications because they are suffering feelings of loss of identity.

Since we are dealing with a psychiatric problem that has medical ramifications, consultation with a highly qualified psychiatrist is the best route. A psychiatrist is a physician. He understands the secondary medical aspects of the condition. He is conversant with medicine so that consultation with other specialists (especially internists) is natural and fruitful for him. More important, he is trained in the treatment of neurotic conditions and obesity is a neurotic condition. Perhaps the patient would do well in a group analytic situation or perhaps in individual treatment; this would depend largely on the patient in question. The psychiatrist is best qualified to make that determination.

In my opinion, the best psychiatric consultation is with a man who is the most highly trained. To me, this is the psychiatrist who has also been trained psychoanalytically. He will be a member of either the American Academy of Psychoanalysis or the American Psychoanalytic Association. This membership indicates that he has been trained and graduated from a psychoanalytic institute recognized by either or both of these qualifying professional organizations. While there are psychiatrists who are particularly interested in problems of obesity, other analytically trained psychiatrists can be just as effective. Psychoanalytic psychotherapy is the treatment of choice, and psychiatrists who are also psychoanalysts are trained to apply that treatment. This is a treatment that works from the bottom up.

This is similar to what goes on in the skilled internist's treatment of the patient who complains of a cough. He doesn't just support him by making him more comfortable with a cough-reducing medicine. He listens to his chest and he X-rays it if need

be. If there is a lesion—from pneumonia or
TB, for example—he treats it with the
necessary medicine. When he has removed
the lesion or cause of the symptoms, he has
undermined the cough, which is now gone
or is of minor consequence and easily
eradicated. The psychoanalyst knows that
removal of hidden fears will result in removal of fat and that removal of fat will help
reveal and resolve more and more problems,
resulting in growth in a healthy direction.
The analyst is interested in removing the
cause of the symptoms, in changing the basic
sick ways of relating, and, in so doing,
removing the need for the symptoms. He is
interested in giving support, but he is even
more interested in healthy, real change.

24

STUFFED CHILDREN

I want to close this section with this short
chapter on prophylaxis. The best prophylaxis is that which begins very early in
life—from the first day, actually. Children
"learn" before they can talk—they are often
better attuned to our feelings than we are.
They learn by identification, imitation,
example, and instruction. Children are like
supersensitive tape-recorders—sponging it

all up, storing it all away, and eventually using it—and we cannot fool them. They read beyond our words to what we feel and what we do. Therefore, the best and most realistic prophylaxis is healthy change in ourselves and in our household environment. An environment that is neither overbearing nor overprotective, that permits individuality of expression and development, that encourages the development and expression of all feelings is invaluable.

The more we can honestly devaluate the food-eating orientation in the household, the better it will be for our children. Food must be devalued as a prime reward and as a celebration substance. It is good for children to partake in social events that are not food-glutting enterprises. Food and weight ought not to be chronic subjects of continuous conversation. Establishing normally small eating quantities from earliest childhood will be infinitely more effective than constant harassments about overweight later on.

If a child seems to be heading toward obesity, then ask yourself if and how you are contributing to this picture. What is your obese state? Do you understand? Do you chastise him about eating too much and then serve him huge portions and fill the refrigerator and cookie jar with all kinds of "poison" goodies? You must be very careful lest you make him the family fat center of attention and an invalid of privileged position. Obviously, it is best not to talk to relatives about your child's weight. Can you genuinely encourage him to get and stay thin by accepting changes in him and his growing up in general, as well as his emancipation from you and the immediate household? If he needs professional help, will you get it for him?

Again, anything you do for your own health will contribute to the health of your child's environment. This is the best means of breaking the obese generation-to-generation chain reaction.

Please: Don't stuff your children!

PART IV

WHAT YOU SHOULD KNOW ABOUT YOURSELF

AN EXERCISE

This section consists of questions that serve to review some important highlights. They are also an exercise designed to stimulate, open up, and extend insight. Please ask and answer them slowly, thoughtfully, and carefully.

Are you overweight? Thin? True thin? Obese thin?

Were you ever overweight? For how long? How much overweight? Are you obese?

When you go to the movies or to see a play and you can't talk, do you make sure you have some candy, nuts, gum, a cigar—something, anything to chew on?

Have you ever calculated the total number of pounds you have lost in your life?

How often do you weigh yourself?

How large were the portions your mother served you?

How large are the portions you eat today?

Would you walk a mile for a "good restaurant"?

In your opinion, does a really good restaurant always serve very large portions?

Do you find yourself judging people by the food they serve? This is tricky. You may not be aware that you do this. But think of a few people. Now think of how you feel about them. Now think about the food they serve.

Did you have a good time at the last wedding you attended? What are your criteria?

How do you chew your food? Comfortably? Lovingly? Angrily? To get it down as rapidly as possible? To fill up what?

When is the last time you you got angry? Did you know it right away? Did you let anyone else know it right away? How was your food intake just after that event?

When you get depressed, does it affect your appetite? How?

Are you trying to be anybody's nice roly-poly chubby-wubby? If so, whose?

Do you know that your family and friends will sometimes see your psychiatrist as a potential adversary? They see themselves as fighting over the *booty:* You. But do you know that these friends and relatives are sicker and more threatened by your potential emancipation and a change in status quo than you are?

Have you thought about this inane possibility—that you may actually fear thinness?

What does thinness mean to you?

Do you know that even though you may feel different about yourself, you don't have to make big, immediate changes just because you are thin?

Do you know that some of these changes have already taken place anyway, and that you've come through all right?

Are you aware that stopping excessive eating is the equivalent of breaking up and destroying resignation?

Do you know the difference between cure and control?

Does it have to be all or nothing or does control hold some attraction for you?

Are you aware that people unconsciously keep themselves unaware of certain problems they have because they don't dare hurt their pride and because they have a fear of giving up the problems in question? Have you considered that recognition of a problem and owning up to it are the first steps in resolving it?

Is vanity more important to you than health?

Is what other people think more important to you than happiness?

Are you a child stuffer? Were you a stuffed child? Are you a stuffed adult? What kind of symbolic "stuff" is food to you? Does it add to your feeling of substantiality?

Do you feel that you would just float away if you lost weight? Are there any other possible means and ways to feel more substantial? Would increased self-esteem do it? Are you the known real owner of any of your assets and accomplishments? Do you own your sense of humor, intelligence, education, and skills, for example, so that they are a source of self-esteem and strength, or are you out of touch with them? Do you take them for granted?

Do you allow yourself to feel love, warmth, anger, sweetness, beauty, jealousy, envy, hurt, gladness or sadness, or are you ashamed of your feelings and out of touch with them?

Do you know that a phobia is defined as an irrational fear? It is not really so much irrational as it is that we just don't discern the rationale. Do you have any phobias—fear of heights, closed places, getting and staying thin?

Do you know you can be afraid to become thin? That you may just touch upon it, as you would a hot stove, and then pull away because staying thin is too frightening and painful? Have you thought about investigating this fear so as to be able to live with sustained thinness? Of course, the assumption here is that you really *know* that you fear thinness.

Do you agree that overweight is a symptom of obesity, which is a conglomerate neurotic attitude, most of which is unconscious?

Do you know anyone who is deathly afraid of disturbing the family status quo?

Do you know anybody who is afraid of sexual feelings and who overeats every time she has a sexual urge or temptation?

How well do you tolerate temptation, frustration, conflict, anxiety, turbulence, confusion? Do you respond to these by eating?

Do you have to immediately satisfy all of your appetites, desires, and seeming needs? Can you wait? Can you practice waiting? Can you learn to wait?

Are you a secret martyr?

Do you feel lovable? Have you over-invested the importance of your lovability quotient?

Would you like to be thin without

changing anything else in your life? Do you think it is possible? Isn't this what most overweight people do, failure after failure after failure?

Do you get up during the night to eat? Have you considered having a psychoanalytic, psychiatric consultation?

Are you aware that resignation and surrender to sickness are not passive? It takes much energy to maintain a resigned status-quo paralysis. Are you aware that people don't ever "just drift into overeating?" It is a very active process that takes great energy and enormous neurotic motivation.

Do you see the world divided into a thin and fat world—heaven and hell? Wise up. Thinness is not the way to enter heaven, but it can lead to a healthier, more fruitful existence.

Are you aware of the cyclic nature of the obese syndrome: Fat-thin-fat-thin-fat?

Does food in your mouth create a taste and desire for more food? Are you prepared to confront addiction withdrawal symptoms?

As fat melts, memories and feelings are freed. Do you know this? Will you be open to owning up to and making use of them?

Are you a family fat center of attraction, in

a privileged invalid position? What is your family position? Are you contributing to being a dehumanized family conversation piece? How?

Are you the unwitting victim of a double-bind fat trap? "I hate you for being fat, but I'll hate you for getting thin and rocking the boat. Maybe you will become too attractive and I'll lose you."

Do you unconsciously put your spouse to the neurotic fat test? Love me, love my fat!

Can stuffing cause a child to be emotionally castrated (that is, to have his self-esteem destroyed) and made to be utterly dependent so that he never emotionally leaves home?

Are you from the willpower school or the insight school? Do you know that increased insight is the only effective way to increase willpower?

Do you eat whole portions set before you regardless of size of the portion or do you frequently leave some?

Have you been on a binge so long that you don't know a binge from normal eating?

Are you aware that the ostensible fear of getting fat again when you are thin can be due largely to a desire to get fat and to go back to old, sick, familiar ways? This can come about if one has not adequately worked out the fear of staying thin and all that it implies.

Are you aware that it is best to work on insight before commencing a weight-reducing regime as well as during and after it?

How can you work with anxiety if you don't know it's there? How can you know it is there if you quickly "eat it away"?

Do you encourage or discourage friends from seeking therapy?

Do you go in for fad diets?

Are you afraid of being the helpless skinny child you once were? Any idea as to factors involved in the composition of your current images?

Can you make a list of your "vulnerables"?

Do you feel different ways about different foods?

Can you make a list of possible things food may mean to you?

If you don't have an EEF, have you learned and trained yourself to know not to exceed normal portions?

Can you assert yourself in situations of all kinds? Anytime? Can you say *No?* Can you say, I want? Or do you eat, instead?

Are you aware that for some very sick people, sustaining their present emotional status and weight can be the beginning of constructive movement, because at least they have stopped gaining and are beginning to exercise some measure of control?

Are you quick to chide and condemn your fat spouse or child or friend? Are you just as quick to praise him when he makes progress?

How have you always felt you looked? Look in the mirror: How *do* you look? How would you like to look? Have you over-invested the importance of looks?

When you feel cold, empty, depressed, do you crave the warm feel of warm food? Mama's hot chicken soup—loaded with crackers—with more and more and more to follow?

Do you have a huge appetite? For what, really?

Do you believe in magic?

Do you have two selves? A fat, unfeeling outer man and a man loaded with feelings locked up inside?

Are you familiar with obese excursions? They can be pretty wild. I know people who have traveled to triple their body weight and then back to half their body weight—and *then* back to double again.

What do I mean by fatness being a comprehensive defense as well as glue and cement, and thinness as being a solvent?

Are you familiar with the simple basic vicious cycle—emotional problems = overweight = emotional problems?

Why does fatness = stagnation?

Are you aware that knowing the anatomy of a problem is already a large part of its cure? For example, if we have an allergy we suffer greatly. The great work is to find and know the allergen. Once this is achieved, it is easy to cope with the problem and effect either cure or control—in this case, to avoid the allergen. In obesity, the aim is for the obese person, through insight, to take responsibility for the resolution of many long-standing personal problems.

Does the world owe you anything because you are crippled? Are you an "injustice collector"?

When you go to the refrigerator, are you at all beginning to realize that what you are looking for is not there? Is it getting easier to shut the door? Are your dreams changing?

Are they less anxious, less longing, less to do with symbolic food, too?

Do you tell fat friends that all they have to do is grab hold of themselves and go on a diet? Of course, dieting is the way to lose weight but haven't you rather oversimplified the problem? Would you go to a mental hospital and empty it by telling people to get hold of themselves? Would you tell a man with a severely fractured leg to get hold of himself and walk?

Are you confusing feeling bloated with an EEF?

Are you satisfied in your love life? Of course, this, as with all areas of life, is a question of degree. But do you face these issues or just gloss over them and keep eating?

How do you really feel about your family and each of its members? Have you told yourself recently? Ever?

Do you confuse fatness with femininity and thinness with masculinity?

Can you say, "I am obese," without revulsion or self-hate?

Are you aware that sex is an area that reflects all the other ways in which a person relates?

How susceptible are you to flattery? Are you very suggestible? Do the people you surround yourself with make really constructive suggestions?

If you have a fat child, do you know the difference between nagging and making constructive suggestions?

Have you known anybody who lost weight and subsequently began to form more constructive relationships?

When you look in the mirror, does a roll of fat look like a roll of fat or like a ripple of muscle?

Can you see people as they physically and mentally really are or do you have the habit of both idolizing them and vilifying them, too? Do "the gods have clay feet" for you?

Do you believe that you can die of a stroke or do you somehow feel magically immune from "fat" physical catastrophes?

Are you waiting for other people to do it (anything) for you?

Are you familiar with this cycle: Real interest in self = a struggle for real insight and growth = control = thinness = liberation of assets = real interest in self?

Have you developed any new interest lately? When you are alone are you aware that you are with a person—yourself?

Are you fat and married to a fat man? Are you afraid to get thin and make him jealous? Are you afraid of breaking up the fat "Bobbsey Twin" look? Perhaps you both need help?

When your husband says he is going to diet, do you take him seriously? This time he may mean it and may succeed, and he can use your help.

Have you met anyone who has an obese state of mind, but who has no MH and does have an EEF so that he's never been fat?

Do you know any family whose members are "obesogenic," but who, except for one fat victim, are not fat themselves?

Do you know any family where the entire immediate family unit is an FFCA for its larger peripheral family of more distant relatives?

Do you know a family where all the members are fat but where only one has been designated and treated as the FFCA? Is he the fattest, youngest, thinnest, shyest, most helpless?

Do you think a new job, husband, thinness will solve all of your problems? What other magic do you believe in?

Have you ever gone looking for pound cake at one o'clock in the morning?

Do you know that a person can be obese and an enormously compulsive overeater for years without any experience of over-weight and then suddenly gain weight—lots of it—for the first time in his life? Would you call him *latently fat?*

Can you feel a change in sexiness and your sexual feelings, appetites, and outlook when you gain or lose weight? Are you aware that this is due to a change in feelings about your-self, rather than to any kind of physiological change?

Were you ever thin for a prolonged period of time? Did anything catastrophic happen? Was it really so bad?

Do you feel that if you lose a few pounds, men will be terribly attracted to you? That you will tend to go hog wild? That you will "give in" to all kinds of sexual opportunities? That you will be thrown into all kinds of conflicts? Are you overlooking the possibili-ty of alternative and constructive ways of facing and resolving impulses and conflicts?

Are you stuffing your husband into an oxygen tent?

Are you afraid you will go crazy if you diet, if you break your diet (for too long), if you get angry, if you let go and feel whatever it is you might feel, and tell people what you really feel?

Do you keep a few sweets and other little goodies around the house just in case the kids need a little something?

Is thinness the supreme test? If you fail, men won't fall at your feet; everybody will not instantly love you; you will not be queen of the world?

If you are keeping yourself out of involvement with people, do you realize that you are wasting time?

Do you have confidence in your taste in clothes? Can you hold your own with other people in any area?

Are you aware that fatness "locks in" neurosis—keeps it intact and unconscious, where it is most damaging?

Are you aware that fatness is the result of neurosis, causes misery that causes more fatness that causes more neurosis? That fatness causes misery beyond that which you are aware of?

Do you ever unwittingly load yourself with food in anticipation of possible rejection: Before asking for a job, date, favor? I've known a number of men who ate volumi-

nously before going to bed in order to make
a possible sexual rejection by their wives
more tolerable.

Does food help you to pretend that your
marriage is better than it is, that your job is
better than it is, and so on? Are you tired of
pretending?

Are you aware that hospitalization and
medication can result in weight loss that is
not sustained because there is no change in
one's fear of staying thin?

Do you know that obese people, in the
same way as small children, are highly
cognizant of and responsive to all kinds of
sensations and sensory stimuli? They often
transfer an overflow of sensations from the
mouth to the eyes and ears, *taking in* through
these other senses.

Are you aware that the most important
response to withdrawal of an emotionally
addicting substance is the generation of
anxiety, which results in a myriad of
symptoms?

Have you ever met anyone who got hugely
fat from her day of marriage or from the day
she gave birth to a baby? This may represent
resignation and hopelessness of ever again
attaining an aspired image of being a
glamorous jet-setting princess or some-such.
Marriage to anyone of imagined lower status

would also further resignation and hopelessness.

Do you know any fat people who are like
some alcoholics? "When I get drunk, I get
right down and roll around in the gutter."
"If I can't have the greatest figure in the
world, I'll have the fattest one."

Do you know that fatness can block emotional developments and growth? Fat people
often give up hope of realization of neurotic
desired images and, more important, hope
of attaining realistic goals. Their total
energy goes into the accumulation and
growth of fat, blocking any other constructive growth.

Do you make the neurotic claim that other
people owe it to you to see that you diet? Do
you make the neurotic projection that other
people must change before you can change?
Have you made the neurotic decision that
other people are responsible for your life
and what happens to you?

Are you aware that dieting can be
followed by feelings of severe emotional
deprivation, often even bringing one to the
verge of tears with longing for all the things
that food has always represented?

Do you know anyone who must eat a load
of ice cream every time she feels the need for
sweetening and love? Know anyone who

does the same in a binge of self-hate or when very angry?

Know anyone who in a combined mood of self-hate and emotional deprivation has searched the garbage can for food remnants and eaten them?

Has the thought of some chocolate on a shelf ever kept you awake all night?

Do you tend to be moody or overeat on weekends? Who is home with you on weekends?

To what lengths do you go to be liked and admired?

Do you know that now is not forever and that anxiety, however painful, will pass?

Have you ever made a list of all of your assets?

Have you formed any constructive, interesting, enjoyable relationships lately?

Have you discovered any new interests in recent years or developed a hitherto unknown facet of yourself?

Do you have a fat woman in your family who makes you feel svelte and superior? Are you unconscious of this dynamic and equally unaware that you help to keep her fat?

Are there any enjoyable activities you look forward to that are in no way related to food? Can you celebrate anything at all in ways not connected to food?

Are you an obese thin in danger of becoming an obese fat man or are you an insightful obese thin?

Do you invariably buy clothes several sizes too large, too small? Why?

Do you diet part of every day or all the time?

Can you stand success, failure? Do you gain weight when things go well or when they go badly?

Do you see yourself as you used to be: A fat, helpless, unhappy little boy or as a thin, helpless, inadequate child? How does this "self-feeling" affect you now in your eating? In business? In relation to other people, particularly your family?

What is more important to you: Self-discipline or self-insight or self-value?

Are you surprised at how well some fat men and women dance, speak, work, and so on? Could it be that you are prejudiced?

Think hard! Is it possible that there is somebody whom you unconsciously have a need to keep fat and dependent upon you?

Does your fatness embarrass your children, husband? Is this a way you "get even with them"?

Do you help keep your husband fat and dependent upon you?

Who are your "eating friends"? That is, who are the people with whom contact always leads to binges? It would be interesting to find out how they make you anxious. In *The Winner's Note Book* (Trident Press), I described the constructive value of breaking up destructive relationships.

If you are attempting to diet, are you replacing the food with what it used to symbolize? Are you trying to socialize more, have more real warmth and meaning in your life, getting involved more with people, work, and enjoyable activities? Are you widening your horizons, hitherto constricted by an obese outlook?

Are you unrealistically heroic? If you need an ally, will you get one—regardless of other people and their opinions? Do you have any feeling for the fact that it is your life that is really at stake?

Do you know the difference between destructive struggle and constructive struggle?

Do you know why psychotherapy by an expert can be the really effective means of sustaining weight loss in difficult cases? Do you know the following:

A. That a relationship with a person who "really understands" can be most supportive and effective?

B. That experiencing changes in one's life in any regard—in clarifying old feelings and attitudes and ways of relating, for example—can break through the resistance of hopelessness and can thus promote changes in dieting, too?

C. That having an unbiased expert ally who is not afraid of unfamiliarity and who has no vested interest in maintaining a crippled status quo can provide a formidable approach to thinness indeed?

Do you know that an "eating tantrum" is often a "temper tantrum"?

Have you been nice to yourself lately? Bought any clothes lately? Are you beginning to get your feet wet in the mainstream of living?

*　　　*　　　*

Note that I have not supplied answers to my questions. That would destroy their usefulness. The purpose of these questions, all carefully constructed from a psychiatric point of view, is to compel you to question yourself, dig out your own answers, and thereby arrive at an understanding of the inner forces that induce you to overeat.

Once you understand *why* you overeat, you will at last be in a position to stop gorging yourself. Diets can be supplied by the dozen. Self-understanding is much harder to arrive at, but much more valuable. And *that* is the purpose of this book.